Caribbean Cooking

Caribbean Cooking

DEVINIA SOOKIA

THE
APPLE
PRESS

A QUINTET BOOK

Published by The Apple Press
6 Blundell Street
London N7 9BH

ISBN 1–85076–488–3

This book was designed and produced by
Quintet Publishing Limited
6 Blundell Street
London N7 9BH

Creative Director: Richard Dewing
Designer: Fiona Akehurst
Project Editor: Katie Preston
Editor: Michelle Clark
Editorial Assistant: Anna Briffa
Illustrator: Amanda Green
Photographer: Andrew Sydenham
Home Economy: Cara Hobday and Nicola Fowler

Manufactured by Bright Arts (Pte) Ltd, Singapore.
Printed by Star Standard Industries (Pte) Ltd, Singapore.

DEDICATION
This book is dedicated to the two people who played
an important part in my life – my loving father Gayadeen and
my devoted husband Bashir.

Contents

The Bahamas

ATLA

Cuba

Caicos & Turks Islands

Cayman Islands

GREATER ANTILLES

Haiti

Dominican
Republic

Puerto
Rico

Jamaica

CARIBBEAN SEA

Aruba

Curaçao

St Martin

Islands

Saba

St Eustatius

St Kitts

Nevis

Antigua

Montserrat

Guadeloupe

SSER ANTILLES

Dominica

Martinique

St Lucia

Barbados

St Vincent

Grenada

Tobago

Trinidad

Introduction

When Christopher Columbus reached the Caribbean islands in 1492, he thought he had found the Garden of Eden. He was overwhelmed by the beauty of the Islands: the richness of the vegetation, the variety of fruits, the exotic scented flowers and the singing of the birds.

The chain of Caribbean islands, stretching 2500 miles from the coast of Florida to the northern coast of Venezuela, consists of more than 7000 islands. Some are little more than rocks in the sea, while others are quite big – Cuba being the largest. The next largest island is Hispaniola, which comprises Haiti and the Dominican Republic, followed by Jamaica and Puerto Rico. These 4 islands and some 25 other large ones, such as Trinidad, Guadeloupe, Martinique, Barbados, St Lucia and Antigua, are known as the Caribbean islands, the West Indies or the Antilles (a name given by fourteenth-century Europeans to a group of imaginary islands in the Atlantic).

One of the most exciting aspects of Caribbean culture is its cuisine. In the Caribbean, "creole" is defined as "mixed and born on the islands". Caribbean cooking can thus be termed "creole cuisine". Caribbean dishes are spicy mixtures of meats, fish and vegetables. The exotic fruits of the islands are coconuts, guavas, mangoes, papayas, pineapples, bananas, custard apples, star apples, soursops, mamey apples, shaddock, tamarind, ugli and passion fruits, jackfruits and avocados. Vegetables found on the islands are christophenes, aubergines, pumpkin, okras, plantains, breadfruits and ackee. The peoples of the Caribbean eat a lot of root vegetables such as yams, cassava, sweet potatoes and dasheen. The fruits of the tropical sea are the local spiny lobster, conch, prawns, crabs, kingfish and other exotic seafood.

Caribbean culture and cuisine have been shaped by four waves of settlers that affected all the islands. The Caribbean islands have been influenced by the Amerindians (Arawaks and Caribs), Europeans (Spanish, British, French and Dutch), Africans and Orientals (Indians and Chinese).

Around 2000 years ago, the native inhabitants of the region, the Arawak and the Carib tribes, who originated from Venezuela and Guyana, settled in the Caribbean islands. They were dispersed by European settlers in the form of Spanish

soldiers, English pirates, Dutch merchants, Irishmen, Scotsmen and Frenchmen who left Europe following the voyages of Christopher Columbus. The Europeans later brought African slaves across from the Congo, Guinea and the Gold Coast to work in their Caribbean sugar-cane plantations. The Africans were followed by Orientals who came as indentured servants from China and India.

The first influence on the Caribbean islands was therefore a primitive one. The Amerindians were farmers who grew crops like maize, cassava (which they used to make bread), sweet potatoes, arrowroot, beans and peppers. Others gathered wild fruits such as guavas, pineapples and cashew fruits and fished or hunted. A favourite dish was pepperpot – a mixed meat and vegetable stew. Now pepperpot is made only with mixed meats, hot pepper and cassareep (the boiled juice of grated cassava).

The Amerindians' food was not sufficient for the Europeans, so Columbus asked for flour, meat, oil, vinegar and wine to be sent over from Spain. The Spanish colonists brought with them many fruits, vegetables and crops that, funnily enough, we now associate with the Caribbean, such as

Right *Preparations for a feast, Grenada.*

breadfruit, limes, oranges, mangoes, bananas, coconut, tamarind, sugar-cane, ginger, coffee and rice. Several Spanish dishes still feature in Caribbean cuisine, such as escovitch (pickled fish) and baccalaitos or stamp and go (salt cod fish-cakes). Barbados has retained much of the British influence. Jug jug – a traditional dish served at Christmas – was originally brought to the island by Scottish people exiled after the Monmouth Rebellion in 1685. It is a version of haggis and is made from salted meats, pigeon peas, herbs and ground millet. The islands of Guadeloupe and Martinique are still part of France and, as such, have a strong French flavour to their cuisine. The Dutch have given the Caribbean one of its most interesting dishes – keshy yana (shrimp-filled Edam cheese).

The third wave – the African slaves – also greatly influenced Caribbean cuisine. The slaves brought with them pigeon peas, yams, okra and taro. More importantly, they developed a style of cooking that is the basis of Caribbean cooking today.

As they were given only very small portions of salt meat and salt fish, they started to supplement their diet by growing their

Right *Sunset at Negril, Jamaica.*

own food. As the food given to them had no taste, they found ingenious ways in which to flavour it with seasonings and pungent spices. Today, the main ingredient in the English-speaking islands for a stew is "a bunch of sive", which is spring onions tied in a bunch with parsley, coriander leaves and thyme. The Spanish-speaking islands use "sofrito" – a sauce made from annatto seeds, coriander leaves, green peppers, onions, garlic and tomatoes. Ginger, nutmeg, cloves, allspice, cinnamon and hot pepper are widely used on all the islands. Many of the traditional dishes have survived, such as callaloo – crab and greens soup.

The fourth influence on Caribbean food came in the early 1800s. There was pressure from England on the European colonists to free their slaves and in 1848 and 1838 respectively the French and English colonies granted emancipation to their slaves. Although they were then offered wages for their work, many ex-slaves refused to work in the fields, especially in Trinidad. Plantation owners, desperately needing a labour force, transported large numbers of indentured servants from India and China. As a result, curry gradually became as much a Caribbean dish as it is an Indian one. Roti or dhalpouri is another favourite in Trinidad and Jamaica. Chinese spare ribs, Chinese vegetables and noodles are popular dishes in Trinidad. Maybe this also explains why, despite the variety of vegetables grown in the Caribbean, such as breadfruit, tannia, eddoes, cassava, sweet potatoes and plantains, which are eaten ripe *and* green, rice is also a very important food for many West Indians. It is served at almost every meal with meat, fish and vegetables.

When we talk of Caribbean cuisine the food of Guyana and Surinam has to be included. Although geographically these two countries are in South America, culturally they form part of the Caribbean. Their cuisines are very similar to that of most of the Caribbean islands, though the Oriental influence on the food is as strong as it is in Trinidad.

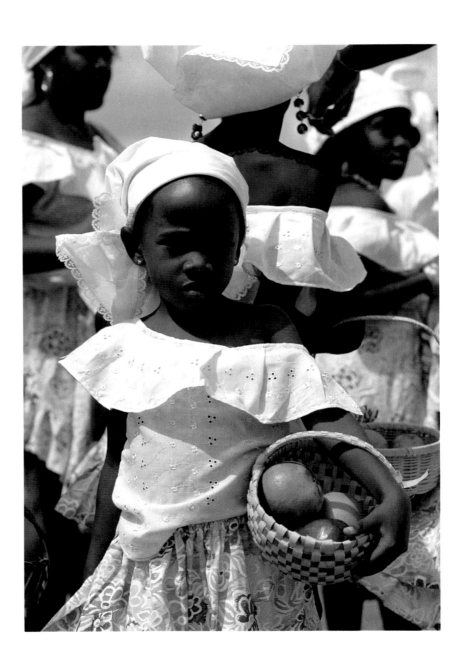

Above *The Willemstad Easter festival, Curaçao.*

Left *Tropical Beach.*

13

Cooks Notes

*N*owadays we see more and more exotic fruits and vegetables in the shops. Plantains, cassava, coconuts, mangoes, avocados, carambolas, guavas, papaya and pineapples can be obtained in any West Indian shop and quite a few are now to be found in supermarkets, too. Even so, it is not always obvious how to recognize, choose and prepare many of these fruits and vegetables, so here are some tips from one who knows.

ACKEE

Ackee is the fruit of an evergreen tree introduced into Jamaica from West Africa. It is reddish-yellow in colour and when ripe it bursts open to display shiny black seeds covered by a creamy-yellow flesh – this is the only edible section and it has a soft texture resembling scrambled eggs. The fruit must *only* be eaten ripe – unripe *and* overripe ackee can be poisonous.

ALLSPICE

This flavouring is also known as pimento seed. It is the dark reddish-brown berry of a tree indigenous to Jamaica. After the berries are dried in the sun, they look like large peppercorns but the scent and flavour are similar to a blend of cinnamon, cloves and nutmeg.

ANNATTO

A rusty red dried seed from the tropical annatto tree. It is used to colour and flavour cooking oil.

ARROWROOT

A white starchy powder obtained from the underground stalk of a plant grown mainly in the Caribbean island of St Vincent. It is used for thickening soups, sauces and stews.

AUBERGINE

Known also as eggplant. Some are large, oval-shaped and purple; others are small and round or small and long with striped purple skin. It is a vegetable which can be cooked on its own or with meat and fish.

AVOCADO

It is commonly known as pear throughout the Caribbean as it is a pear-shaped fruit with creamy flesh and a thick green skin. Avocados can be bought when still firm. If you want to test the ripeness of an avocado, put it in the palm of your hand and squeeze it gently; when it yields to gentle pressure, it is ready to eat.

To prepare an avocado, cut it in half lengthways. Gently twist the halves apart to loosen the stone. Remove the stone with a knife. Rub the exposed flesh with lemon or lime juice to prevent it discolouring.

BAKES

Fried biscuits – a speciality of Trinidad.

BEANS

Islanders use the term peas for both peas and beans. Rice 'n' Peas is a dish made with rice and kidney beans or pigeon peas.

BREADFRUIT

A large round or oval green fruit used as a vegetable. It is best used when the skin is green rather than brown. The central core should be removed and the cream-coloured flesh eaten as a starchy vegetable, boiled, roasted or fried.

CALLALOO

The name given to the leaves of the dasheen or taro plant with which Callaloo is made.

CASHEW

An evergreen tree and shrub native to the West Indies. It bears a reddish, pear-shaped cashew apple from the bottom of which grows the kidney-shaped nut, which is edible only when roasted.

CASSAREEP

This is an essential part of the stew known as pepperpot. It is the juice obtained from grated cassava and flavoured with cinnamon, cloves and brown sugar.

To make 6 tablespoons, you need 850 g/2 lb of young cassava root. Peel the brown bark off with a small sharp knife to reveal the white flesh of the cassava root. Cut the cassava root in half and finely grate half of it into a deep bowl lined with a double thickness of dampened muslin. Bring the ends of the

cloth together to enclose the pulp and twist the cloth very tightly to squeeze the cassava juice into the bowl. Discard the pulp. Grate and squeeze the rest of the cassava in the same way. Pour the liquid into a small frying pan and cook it over a medium heat for about 1 minute, stirring constantly, until the cassareep is smooth and thick. Cassareep is made fresh each time you need it.

CASSAVA

Also known as yuca, manioc, tapioca and mandioca. It is a long irregularly shaped root with a dark brown rough bark-like skin and hard white starchy flesh. It is an important item in the diet of many West Indians and can be eaten boiled, baked or fried.

CHRISTOPHENE

Also known as cho-cho, choyote, chayote and tropical squash. This is a pear-shaped fruit with a single large stone in the centre. The skin varies in colour from white to pale yellow or bright green. The flesh is cooked as a vegetable and tastes like courgette or marrow.

COCONUT

When you buy a coconut, shake it to make sure it has liquid inside – this is a sign that the coconut is fresh.

To open the coconut, puncture two of its "eyes" – the darker dots on one end – with a small, sharp knife or an ice pick. Drain all the liquid from the coconut, then tap the whole surface of the shell lightly with a hammer. Now give the shell a sharp blow with the hammer. This will open the coconut and the meat will now come away from the shell.

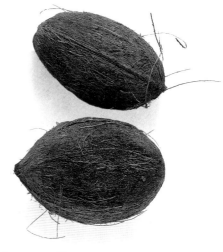

How to make coconut milk

Grate the coconut meat. Measure the coconut and stir in an equal amount of hot, but not boiling, water. Cover a bowl with a piece of muslin and strain the coconut through the cloth, pressing down hard on the coconut with a wooden spoon to extract as much liquid as possible. If you measure 300 ml/10 fl oz of coconut meat to 300 ml/10 fl oz of water, you should produce 300 ml/10 fl oz of coconut milk.

CONCH

Known as lambi in the Caribbean. It is an edible sea snail with big horns.

CORIANDER

Known as Chinese parsley or cilantro. It is an aromatic herb and has a pungent flavour.

CUMIN

It is the yellowish-brown seed of a plant from the parsley family. It is aromatic and is available whole or ground.

DASHEEN

Also known as taro and cocoyam. It is a tropical plant cultivated for both its underground tubers, which are eaten boiled, roasted or baked, and for its large leaves – known as callaloo leaves – which are used in Callaloo. If dasheen leaves are not available, fresh spinach is a good substitute.

15

EDDOES

A root vegetable related to dasheen. The underground tubers are similar and the leaves cannot be eaten.

FLYING FISH

An unusual silver-blue winged fish with a white, slightly salty flesh and a large number of bones. It is found off the coasts of Barbados.

GHEE

Clarified butter – butter with the milk solids removed – that tolerates high temperatures without burning.

HOT PEPPERS

Hot peppers vary in hotness but you must always be very careful when handling them: they can burn your skin and irritate your eyes, so wear rubber gloves when preparing them.

To prepare hot peppers rinse them in cold water, then pull out the stalks, cut them in half and remove the seeds. If the ribs inside the pods are thin, leave them as they are, but if they are firm, remove them with a sharp knife.

To take some of the heat out of hot peppers, soak them in cold, salted water for an hour before using them.

MANGO

The mango is a tropical fruit much used in Caribbean cooking but also delicious eaten raw. The ripe fruit varies in colour from green to bright red. Mangoes are not easy to eat unless you known how to remove the stone. Place the mango flat side down on a board. Cut a thick slice from the top of the fruit as near to the stone as possible. Turn the fruit over. Repeat with the other side. The two halves can then be eaten by scooping out the flesh. The juicy flesh still attached to the stone can be cut off in chunks.

MAWBY BARK

The bark of a tropical tree which has a bitter taste. It is used to make a refreshing drink in the Caribbean.

METHI LEAVES

Also known as fenugreek leaves, methi leaves are taken from a leguminous plant with aromatic seeds.

OKRAS

Known as gumbo, ochro, bamie or lady's fingers, this plant produces pod-like fruits about 10 cm/4 in long. Each pod is oblong in shape and pointed at one end, with a soft and sticky interior. The pod is cooked as a vegetable.

PALM HEART

Tender ivory-coloured shoots obtained from the core at the crown or top of the palm tree. Palm hearts are used as a vegetable or a salad ingredient.

PAPAYA

Also known as pawpaw, this is a large melon-like fruit which ranges in length from 7.5 to 50 cm (3 to 20 in). The fruit has a green skin when raw and a yellow skin, sweet yellow flesh and black seeds when ripe.

The soft skin contains papain, which is a meat tenderizer. A deliciously simple starter is to serve papaya with ginger.

PASSION FRUIT

An egg-shaped fruit about 5 cm/2 in long. When ripe the leathery skin becomes wrinkled and purple in colour. To eat, it must be cut in half and the juicy yellow seeds scooped out with a spoon.

PIGEON PEAS

Known as goongoo or gunga peas. They are the size of a small garden pea. Young pigeon peas are green and are available in tins.

PINEAPPLE

One of the most familiar tropical fruits. The best way to peel a pineapple is to remove the spiky leaves from the top, then make slanting cuts downwards to remove the skin. It can then be sliced or cut into wedges, removing the core, though, if the pineapple is very ripe, the core should not be removed as it has a very good flavour and texture.

PLANTAIN

A fruit of the banana family, similar in shape but larger and not so sweet; it must be cooked before being eaten. It can be green or yellow in colour according to ripeness.

Plantains are difficult to handle as the thick skin clings to the fruit. To remove the peel, cut off the ends of the plantain and then halve the trimmed plantain with a sharp knife. Make four evenly spaced lengthways slits in the skin of each half, cutting through to the flesh from one end to the other. Then, starting at the corner of one slit, lift the skin away, one strip at a time.

SALT BEEF

Beef preserved in salt. It can be eaten in bread or in recipes.

SALT COD

Originally brought to the Caribbean as food for slaves by the Colonists. Of all the salted fish, cod seems to have the best flavour. To remove salt wash well and soak for several hours or overnight in cold water.

SEA EGG

The Island name for a white sea urchin.

SORREL

A tropical flower grown throughout the islands. Its fleshy sepal has a faintly acid taste and is used in making drinks, jams and jellies.

SOURSOP

A large dark green heart-shaped fruit with a spiny skin. Its pithy flesh has black seeds and is slightly acidic. It is often used to make drinks or ice-creams.

SWEET POTATO

A tuberous vegetable whose skin colour ranges from yellow to reddish brown and pink. The flesh may be white, yellow or orange and can be eaten boiled, baked, fried or roasted. Ideal for both sweet and savoury dishes.

TANNIA

A root vegetable of the same family as the dasheen. It is the size of a large baking potato with dark brown bark-like skin. The firm flesh is white and has a nutty flavour.

TARO

Another name for dasheen.

YAM

These are tubers which grow under large vines known as tropical creepers. Although very like the sweet potato, the yam is not as sweet; the flesh is moister in texture and the skin is red or brown.

 17

SEASONING AND MARINATING

Seasoning and marinating are essential in Caribbean cooking. Nothing is cooked without being seasoned a few hours before and left to marinate. Cheap cuts are transformed if they are left to marinate in spices overnight.

~ Except for steak, meats such as beef, pork, veal, lamb, venison, chicken, hare or rabbit must be allowed to marinate for at least 4 hours before cooking.

~ A good marinade for meat is 300 ml/10 fl oz cold water, 2 crushed garlic cloves, generous pinches of salt and freshly ground black pepper, 1 tablespoon vinegar and 1 teaspoon chopped thyme.

~ Fish must be cleaned well in cold water. If it is to be cooked the same day, wash it well with lime or lemon juice under cold running water. If not, wash it with cold water and vinegar. Remove the scales and any remaining traces of blood, then cut it into steaks or fillets or leave whole as required.

~ For the best results, marinate fish for at least 4 hours or overnight. A good marinade for fish is 1 finely chopped spring onion, 1 teaspoon chopped hot pepper, generous pinches of salt and freshly ground black pepper, 1 teaspoon chopped thyme, 1 tablespoon vinegar, 2 whole cloves, 3 crushed garlic cloves and cold water.

Soups

CALLALOO ~ Barbados

PUMPKIN SOUP ~ Antigua

PEPPERPOT ~ Trinidad

BLACK BEAN SOUP ~ Cuba

CHICKEN AND VEGETABLE SOUP ~ Aruba

TOMATO AND SWEET POTATO SOUP ~ Dominica

PEANUT SOUP ~ St Vincent

BREADFRUIT SOUP ~ Grenada

SOPITO ~ Curaçao

GREEN PIGEON PEA SOUP ~ Puerto Rico

Barbados

Callaloo

Crab and Greens Soup

SERVES 6

225 g/ 8oz dasheen leaves
or 450 g/1 lb fresh spinach
40 g/1½ oz butter or margarine
1 onion, finely chopped
2 garlic cloves, crushed
1 fresh hot pepper, deseeded and finely chopped
(see page 16)
100 g/4 oz okra, trimmed and sliced
1 sprig fresh thyme
900 ml/1½ pt chicken stock
300 ml/10 fl oz coconut milk (see page 15)
salt and freshly ground black pepper
225 g/8 oz crabmeat, fresh, tinned or frozen
dash of hot pepper sauce

~ Wash the dasheen or spinach leaves, drain and then shred them.

~ Heat the butter or margarine in a large saucepan over a medium heat. Add the onion and garlic and cook for 5 minutes, stirring occasionally until soft and golden. Add the hot pepper, okra and thyme and cook for 5 more minutes, stirring constantly. Stir in the dasheen or spinach leaves and cook for 3 minutes, turning them in the pan to ensure they are evenly cooked. Pour over the stock and coconut milk, season with salt and freshly ground black pepper and bring to the boil. Then lower the heat, cover the pan and simmer for 30 minutes.

~ Add the crabmeat and cook for 5 more minutes until it has heated through. Taste and adjust the seasoning if necessary and stir in the pepper sauce.

~ Serve on its own in warmed soup bowls or with Cornmeal Dumplings.

Pumpkin Soup

SERVES 4–6

850 g/2 lb pumpkin, peeled, deseeded and cut into
2.5 cm/1 in cubes
salt and freshly ground black pepper
25 g/1 oz butter or margarine
1 large onion, finely chopped
3 spring onions, trimmed and finely chopped
3 tomatoes, skinned and chopped
250 ml/8 fl oz coconut milk (see page 15)
¼ tsp freshly grated nutmeg
pinch of cayenne pepper
150 ml/5 fl oz soured cream or yogurt

~ Put the pumpkin in a saucepan and add enough water (about 900 ml/1½ pt) to cover, together with 1 teaspoon of salt. Bring to the boil, then lower the heat and simmer for 20 minutes.

~ Drain and reserve the cooking liquid.

~ Melt the butter or margarine in a clean saucepan over moderate heat. Add the onion and spring onions and fry them, stirring constantly, for 5 minutes, until they are soft and golden. Add the pumpkin, tomatoes, coconut milk, 750 ml/1¼ pt of the pumpkin cooking liquid, half the nutmeg, a pinch of cayenne pepper and salt and freshly ground black pepper. Bring to the boil, then lower the heat, cover and simmer for 30 minutes.

~ Remove the pan from the heat and leave it to cool slightly. Liquidize half the soup at a time in a blender, then return it to the pan. Heat it through for 5 minutes, then pour the soup into warmed soup bowls and swirl a little of the soured cream or yogurt on top. Sprinkle with the remaining nutmeg and serve at once.

Trinidad

Pepperpot

Chicken and Meat Stew

SERVES 6 TO 8

1.5 kg/3 lb boiling chicken, trimmed of fat and cut into
12 pieces
225 g/8 oz fresh pig's trotter
1.9 l/3¼ pt water
1½ tsp salt
1.5 kg/3 lb boned pork or beef cut into 5 cm/2 in cubes
6 tbsp cassareep (see page 15)
1 large onion, sliced
1½ tbsp brown sugar
2 whole, fresh hot peppers
4 whole cloves
5 cm/2 in piece of cinnamon stick
¼ tbsp dried thyme
2½ tsp malt vinegar

~ Put the chicken, pig's trotter and water into a large saucepan (the water should cover them by 2.5 cm/1 in). Add the salt and bring to the boil over a low heat, skimming off any foam as it collects on the surface. Then, reduce the heat, partially cover the pan and simmer for about 1 hour or until the chicken is cooked.

~ Skim as much fat as possible from the surface of the soup. Stir in the pork or beef, cassareep, onion, brown sugar, hot peppers, cloves, cinnamon stick and thyme and bring to the boil over a high heat. Lower the heat and simmer for 30 minutes, stirring occasionally, until the meat is cooked.

~ Remove the cloves, cinnamon stick and hot peppers, stir in the vinegar and taste, adjusting the seasoning if necessary.

~ Serve the soup with boiled yam, cassava or potatoes as accompaniments.

23

Black Bean Soup

SERVES 6

675

450 g/1 lb dried black beans
2½ tsp salt

1350

900 ml/1½ pt chicken stock
1½ tbsp vegetable oil mixed with 1 tsp liquid annatto
(see page 14)
1 medium onion, finely chopped
1 fat garlic clove, finely chopped

350   225 g/8 oz lean cooked ham, finely chopped
1 large, firm, ripe tomato, peeled, deseeded and finely
chopped or 225 g/8 oz tin chopped tomatoes, drained
1½ tbsp malt vinegar
½ tsp ground cumin
freshly ground black pepper

24

~Wash the beans under cold running water and drain in a colander. Put the beans in a large saucepan together with the salt and enough water to cover the beans by 5 cm/2 in. Bring to the boil over a high heat, then reduce the heat, partially cover the pan and simmer for 2 hours or until the beans are tender.

~Drain the beans, reserving the liquid, and leave them on one side to cool.

~Add enough chicken stock to the reserved cooking liquid from the beans to make 1.2 l/2 pt. Put half the cooked beans in a blender and grind, but not too finely. Grind the remaining beans. Mix the ground beans with the chicken and bean stock.

~Heat the oil in a large saucepan and add the onion and garlic and cook for 5 minutes, stirring frequently. Stir in the ham, tomato, vinegar, cumin, bean and stock mixture and freshly ground black pepper to taste. Bring to the boil, then lower the heat and simmer for 15 minutes. Taste to check the seasoning, adjusting if necessary.

~Serve the soup in bowls, together with slices of fresh bread.

Chicken and Vegetable Soup

SERVES 6

1.5 kg/3 lb chicken, cut into 8 pieces
2.75 l/5 pt chicken stock
4 large tomatoes, peeled, deseeded and chopped or
2 × 450 g/1 lb tins chopped tomatoes, drained
2 medium-sized corn cobs, cut into 7.5 cm/3 in pieces
2 medium yams, peeled and chopped into
2.5 cm/1 in thick slices
2 small potatoes, peeled and cut into
2.5 cm/1 in thick slices
100 g/4 oz pumpkin, peeled and diced
75 g/3 oz fresh or frozen green peas
2 small hot peppers, deseeded and sliced thinly
(see page 16)
2½ tsp salt
freshly ground black pepper
1½ tbsp finely chopped fresh chives

~Put the chicken pieces and stock into a large saucepan and bring to the boil over a high heat. Skim off the foam with a large spoon, then reduce the heat, partially cover and simmer for 45 minutes.

~Skim the fat from the soup. Add the tomatoes, corn, yams, potatoes, pumpkin, peas, hot peppers, salt and freshly ground black pepper and bring to the boil. Reduce the heat and simmer for about 20 minutes or until the chicken and vegetables are cooked.

~Taste the soup, adjusting the seasoning if necessary. Stir in the chives, then serve at once.

Tomato and Sweet Potato Soup

Peanut Soup

SERVES 6

1 tbsp oil
15 g/½ oz butter or margarine
2 onions, finely chopped
225 g/8 oz sweet potatoes, peeled and diced
450 g/1 lb tomatoes, skinned and finely chopped
600 ml/1 pt chicken stock
1 tsp salt
1 tsp chopped fresh thyme
juice and grated rind of 1 orange
juice and grated rind of 1 lemon or lime
freshly ground black pepper
slices of lemon, orange and tomato to garnish

~ Heat the oil and butter or margarine in a large saucepan. Add the onions and cook them until they are soft.

~ Add the sweet potatoes, tomatoes, chicken stock, salt, thyme, orange juice and rind, lemon or lime juice and rind and freshly ground black pepper to taste. Bring to the boil, then lower the heat, cover the saucepan and simmer for 25 minutes.

~ Liquidize the soup in a blender, then return it to the saucepan and simmer for 5 more minutes to heat it through.

~ Serve it in warmed soup bowls, garnished with a slice of tomato, orange and lemon.

SERVES 4

50 g/2 oz butter or margarine
1 onion, grated
1 celery stick, chopped
1 garlic clove, crushed
1 sprig fresh thyme, chopped
1 tbsp flour
900 ml/1½ pt chicken stock
100 g/4 oz crunchy peanut butter or 275 g/10 oz coarsely ground peanuts
475 ml/16 fl oz milk
2 tsp salt
½ tsp freshly ground black pepper
¼ green pepper, deseeded and chopped

~ Melt the butter or margarine in a large saucepan over a low heat. Add the onion, celery, garlic and thyme. Cook for 5 minutes, stirring all the time, then add the flour and stock, gradually, stirring. Increase the heat, then stir in the peanut butter or peanuts and cook for 10 minutes.

~ Reduce the heat and add the milk, salt and pepper. Simmer for 15 minutes.

~ Serve very hot, garnished with the chopped green pepper.

Right *Peanut soup.*

Grenada

Breadfruit Soup

SERVES 6

50 g/2 oz butter or margarine
1 medium onion, finely chopped
1 fat garlic clove, crushed
175 g/6 oz fresh breadfruit, peeled, cored and chopped
600 ml/1 pt chicken stock
300 ml/10 fl oz single cream
1 tsp salt
¼ tsp freshly ground black pepper
2 tsp finely chopped fresh parsley

~ Melt the butter or margarine in a large saucepan. Add the onion and garlic and cook for 5 minutes, stirring until they are soft. Add the breadfruit and chicken stock and bring to the boil. Reduce the heat and simmer for 20 minutes or until the breadfruit is tender.

~ Put half the mixture in a blender, together with half of the cream, and blend them together. Tip the purée into a bowl. Repeat for the remainder of the mixture, using the remainder of the cream. Season the creamy purée with the salt and pepper. Chill the soup and sprinkle with chopped parsley before serving.

28

Curaçao

Sopito

Fish and Coconut Soup

SERVES 6

2 onions
1 garlic clove
2 bay leaves
1 celery stick, chopped
1 leek, chopped
1 tsp whole peppercorns
1 tbsp finely chopped fresh basil
1 tsp cumin seeds
1 tsp salt
1.2 l/2 pt cold water
450 g/1 lb whole fish (sea bream, red snapper or mullet),
cleaned and scaled
100 g/4 oz salt beef, diced
2 whole cloves
1 fresh hot pepper, sliced (see page 16)
300 ml/10 fl oz coconut milk (see page 15)
3 tbsp cornmeal
225 g/8 oz unshelled prawns
1 tbsp finely chopped fresh basil, to garnish

~Slice one of the onions and put the slices in a saucepan with the garlic, bay leaves, celery, leek, peppercorns, basil, cumin seeds and 1 teaspoon salt. Pour over 1.2 l/2 pt cold water.

~Bring to the boil over a moderate heat, then lower the heat, cover and simmer for 15 minutes.

~Add the fish and cook for 10 to 15 minutes until the fish flakes easily when tested with a fork.

~Remove the pan from the heat and sieve the stock into a clean pan. Reserve the fish.

~Finely chop the second onion and add it to the fish stock, together with the diced beef, cloves, hot pepper and coconut milk.

~Bring to the boil over a moderate heat, then lower the heat, cover and simmer for 45 minutes until the beef is tender, removing the hot pepper 15 minutes into this time and discarding it.

~Sprinkle over the cornmeal and cook for 2 minutes, stirring constantly.

~Skin and bone the fish and cut the flesh into 2.5 cm/1 in pieces. Add the fish and prawns to the soup and cook over a low heat for 5 minutes.

~Serve in warmed soup bowls, garnished with the fresh, chopped basil.

29

Puerto Rico

Green Pigeon Pea Soup

SERVES 6

100 g/4 oz butter or margarine
1 medium onion, finely chopped
1 fat garlic clove, crushed
1 large, firm tomato, peeled, deseeded and chopped
1 small green pepper, deseeded, white pith removed and
finely chopped
100 g/4 oz cooked boned chicken, diced
450 g/1 lb fresh pumpkin, peeled, deseeded and diced

600 ml/1 pt chicken stock
450 g/1 lb tin green pigeon peas with liquid
salt and freshly ground black pepper

~Melt the butter or margarine in a large saucepan and fry the onion and garlic over a moderate heat until they are soft.

~Add the tomato, green pepper and chicken, cover the pan and simmer for 5 minutes.

~Add the pumpkin, chicken stock and green pigeon peas and bring to the boil. Reduce the heat and simmer for 20 minutes or until the soup thickens and the pumpkin is tender.

~The soup should be lumpy. Season to taste with salt and freshly ground black pepper and serve at once.

Starters and Snacks

CHEESE CORN STICKS ~ Puerto Rico

STAMP AND GO ~ Jamaica

PRAWN AND POTATO CAKES ~ Dominican Republic

BEEF PATTIES ~ Jamaica

OYSTER COCKTAIL ~ Grenada

CHICKEN AND RICE CROQUETTES ~ Antigua

PALM HEART SALAD ~ Martinique

ESCOVITCH ~ Barbados

BULJOL ~ Trinidad

Cheese Corn Sticks

MAKES 24

600 ml/1 pt water
1 tsp salt
175 g/6 oz yellow cornmeal
50 g/2 oz Edam or Cheddar, grated
vegetable oil for frying

~ Bring the water, with the salt added, to the boil in a saucepan. Gradually add the cornmeal, stirring constantly. Continue to stir for 10 minutes until the mixture is thick.

~ Remove the saucepan from the heat. Add the grated cheese and mix it in well, then leave the mixture to cool.

~ Wetting your hands in cold water from time to time, make the mixture into sticks about 7.5 cm/3 in long and 2.5 cm/1 in wide. Lay them on greaseproof paper and chill for 3 hours or for a day.

~ When ready to fry, preheat the oven to its lowest temperature and line a baking dish with kitchen foil.

~ Heat a little vegetable oil in a frying pan and fry 4 sticks at a time, turning them over and cooking them until they are crisp. Transfer the cooked sticks to the baking dish and keep them warm in the oven while you fry the rest. Serve them hot.

Stamp and Go

Cod Fish-cakes

MAKES 24

225 g/ 8oz salt cod
2 tbsp vegetable oil mixed with 1 tsp liquid annatto
(see page 14)
1 medium onion, finely chopped
100 g/4 oz flour
1 tsp baking powder
¹/₂ tsp salt
1 egg, lightly beaten
135 ml/4¹/₂ fl oz milk
2¹/₂ tsp melted butter or margarine
¹/₂ fresh hot pepper, finely chopped (see page 16)
vegetable oil for frying

~ Soak the salt cod in a glass bowl for 12 hours, changing the water 3 or 4 times during this time.

~ Drain the cod, rinse it under cold running water and then put it into a large saucepan and cover with fresh cold water. Bring to the boil, then reduce the heat and simmer for 20 minutes.

~ Drain off the water and lift out the fish. Remove the skin and bones and flake the fish.

~ Heat the annatto-flavoured oil in a clean large saucepan. Add the onion and cook until soft.

~ Remove the pan from the heat and set to one side.

~ Sift the flour, baking powder and salt into a large mixing bowl. Add the egg, milk and melted butter or margarine and mix together. Add the cooked onion and oil, the flaked cod and the hot pepper. Mix together to form a batter.

~ Pour vegetable oil to a 1-cm/¹/₂-in depth into a large frying pan and heat until very hot. Drop the batter, a tablespoon at a time, into the hot oil, and fry for 3 minutes, turning the fish-cakes over so they cook evenly. Drain on kitchen paper. These fish-cakes can be eaten hot or cold.

33

Prawn and Potato Cakes

MAKES 14

2 medium baking potatoes, peeled and quartered
75 g/3 oz butter or margarine
100 g/4 oz Cheddar cheese, grated
1 egg yolk
3 tbsp finely chopped fresh parsley
1 tsp salt
freshly ground black pepper
1 medium onion, finely chopped
450 g/1 lb cooked shelled prawns, deveined and chopped
50 g/2 oz flour
1 egg, lightly beaten
25 g/1 oz soft, fresh, white breadcrumbs
vegetable oil for frying

~Boil the potatoes in salted water until they are soft.

~Drain and mash the potatoes with a fork. Add two thirds of the butter or margarine, the cheese, egg yolk, parsley, salt and freshly ground black pepper to taste. Mix well until the mixture is smooth.

~Melt the remaining butter or margarine in a frying pan. Add the onion and cook for 5 minutes, then add the prawns and cook for 1 minute.

~Add the contents of the frying pan to the potato mixture and mix together well. Chill the mixture and form it into round shapes, approximately 4 cm/1½ in in diameter, with your hands and roll each one in flour and brush with the beaten egg. Dip each in the breadcrumbs and put the finished cakes on greaseproof paper.

~Deep fry 5 cakes at a time, turning them over when they are golden. Drain them on kitchen paper and serve them hot or cold.

34

Above *Beach with palms, Anguilla.*

Jamaica

Beef Patties

MAKES 12

FOR THE PASTRY
450 g/1 lb plain flour
2 tsp turmeric
1 tsp salt
225 g/8 oz butter, softened, or margarine
3 tbsp cold water

FOR THE FILLING
2 tbsp vegetable oil
1 onion, finely chopped
2 spring onions, finely chopped
2 garlic cloves, crushed
2 fresh hot peppers, deseeded and finely chopped
350 g/12 oz minced beef
4 tomatoes, skinned and chopped
¼ tsp turmeric
¼ tsp ground cumin
¼ tsp ground ginger

¼ tsp ground cinnamon
¼ tsp ground cloves
¼ ground cardamom
240 ml/8 fl oz water
salt and freshly ground black pepper

FOR THE GLAZE
2 egg yolks, beaten

~ First make the pastry. Sift the flour, turmeric and salt into a bowl. Add the butter or margarine and mix well until the mixture resembles breadcrumbs. Mix in just enough of the cold water to form a stiff dough. Wrap the dough in cling film and chill for 2 hours.

~ For the filling, heat the oil in a medium saucepan and fry the onion until it is soft. Add the spring onions, garlic and hot peppers and cook for 2 more minutes.

~ Add the beef, tomatoes and spices and season to taste with salt and freshly ground black pepper. Reduce the heat, stir in 120 ml/4 fl oz of water and cook for 20 minutes.

~ Remove the pan from the heat and leave the mixture to cool.

~ Meanwhile, preheat the oven to 200°C/ 400°F/Gas Mark 6. Roll out the pastry and cut out 12 circles approximately 18 cm/7 in in diameter using a saucer.

~ Put 2 tablespoons of the filling on one side of the circle, then fold the other half over so the edges meet. Crimp the edges together with a fork to seal. Place them on a baking tray lined with kitchen foil and brush the tops with the beaten egg yolk glaze. Bake in the centre of the oven for 30 minutes until golden brown. Serve at once.

37

Grenada

Oyster Cocktail

SERVES 6

24 fresh oysters
4 tsp lime juice
½ tsp hot pepper sauce
1 onion, finely chopped
2 tsp salt
1 small, fresh tomato, skinned and finely chopped
1 tsp olive oil

~ Rinse the oysters under cold running water, then leave them to soak in a bowl of cold water with 1 teaspoon of the lime juice for 5 minutes. Drain off the water.

~ In a bowl, mix the remaining lime juice with the hot pepper sauce, onion, salt, tomato and olive oil. Add the oysters and leave to marinate for 5 minutes.

~ Chill for 10 minutes before serving.

Left Beef Patties

Chicken and Rice Croquettes

MAKES 24

450 g/1 lb cooked, diced chicken
450 g/1 lb cooked rice
½ onion, chopped
2 tsp tomato ketchup
salt and freshly ground black pepper
½ tsp paprika
3 eggs, beaten
100 g/4 oz breadcrumbs
vegetable oil for frying

~ Mix all the ingredients together, except the eggs, breadcrumbs and oil. Roll the mixture into small balls, then dip each one in the beaten egg and roll in the breadcrumbs to coat them.

~ Heat some oil in a saucepan and deep-fry the croquettes until they are golden brown. Serve at once with hot pepper sauce on the side.

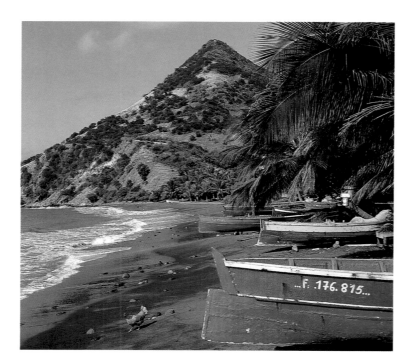

Above *Fishing boats, Martinique.*

Palm Heart Salad

SERVES 6

100 g/4 oz tin palm hearts, drained
2 green mangoes, peeled and thinly sliced
½ cucumber, peeled and thinly sliced
2 ripe avocado pears
½ fresh hot pepper, deseeded and thinly sliced
(see page 16)

FOR THE DRESSING
juice of 1 lime or lemon
1 tsp mustard powder
1 tsp sugar
4 tbsp olive oil
salt and freshly ground black pepper

~ First make the dressing. Mix half the lime or lemon juice with the mustard powder, sugar, olive oil and salt and freshly ground black pepper.

~ Next, make the salad. Chop the palm hearts into slices. Put the palm heart slices, mango and cucumber into a glass serving bowl. Peel, stone and thinly slice the avocados and add them to the bowl. Stir in the hot pepper together with the rest of the lime or lemon juice to prevent the ingredients discolouring.

~ Serve the salad with the dressing on the side.

Right *Palm Heart Salad.*

Barbados

Escovitch

Pickled Fish

SERVES 6

4 onions, thinly sliced
2 carrots, scraped and sliced
2 green peppers, deseeded and chopped
2 bay leaves
1/2 tsp fresh hot pepper, crushed (see page 16)
2 tsp salt
freshly ground black pepper
6 tbsp white wine vinegar
5 tbsp olive oil
300 ml/10 fl oz cold water
850 g/2 lb red snapper, skinned and filleted

~Put the onions, carrots, green peppers, bay leaves, hot pepper, salt and freshly ground black pepper to taste, plus the vinegar, 1½ tablespoons of the oil and the water into a large saucepan and bring to the boil over a high heat. Reduce the heat and simmer until the vegetables are cooked.

~Meanwhile, pour the remaining oil into a large frying pan and heat. Add the fish fillets and cook each side for 2 minutes or until golden brown. Transfer the fish to a shallow heatproof dish. Pour the contents of the saucepan over the fish and leave to cool.

~Serve with baked yams or breadfruit.

Left *Escovitch.*

Trinidad

Buljol

Salt Cod Salad

SERVES 6

225 g/ 8oz salt cod, soaked overnight and drained
juice of 1 lime or lemon
1 onion, finely chopped
3 tomatoes, chopped
3 tbsp olive oil
2 hard-boiled eggs, chopped
1 fresh hot pepper, deseeded and finely chopped
(see page 16)
2 tbsp finely chopped spring onions
1 green pepper, deseeded and finely chopped
2 tbsp finely chopped fresh parsley
freshly ground black pepper

~Boil the cod for 20 minutes or until it flakes.

~Drain off the water and rinse under cold running water. Remove the skin and bones and flake the fish. Put the flaked fish into a glass bowl, add the lime or lemon juice, onion, tomatoes, olive oil, eggs, hot pepper, spring onions, green pepper, parsley and freshly ground black pepper and mix well.

~When the mixture has cooled, cover the bowl with cling film and refrigerate overnight.

~Serve the next day on crackers, fresh bread or small, toasted slices of bread.

Chicken Dishes

CARIB-ORIENT CHICKEN ~ Guyana

CALYPSO CHICKEN ~ Jamaica

MARINATED FRIED CHICKEN ~ Dominican Republic

CHICKEN AND RICE STEW ~ Puerto Rico

POULET ROTI À LA CRÉOLE ~ Haiti

CORIANDER CHICKEN ~ Trinidad

CHICKEN AND NOODLE BAKE ~ Guyana

SWEET AND SPICY CHICKEN ~ Grenada

POULET AU JARDINIÈRE ~ Guadeloupe

Guyana

Carib-Orient Chicken

SERVES 4

1.5 kg/3 lb chicken, cut into 5 cm/2 in pieces
120 ml/4 fl oz soy sauce
2 tbsp brown sugar
2 garlic cloves, crushed
1 tbsp grated fresh ginger root
3 tbsp white wine

~ Wash the chicken pieces and put them in a bowl.

~ Combine the remaining ingredients in a large saucepan and stir over a medium heat until the sugar has dissolved. Leave to cool.

~ Pour the sauce over the chicken and leave to marinate for 5 hours.

~ Grill the chicken pieces until they are tender and serve.

44

Jamaica

Calypso Chicken

SERVES 6

1.5 kg/3 lb chicken, cut into 5 cm/2 in pieces
1/2 lemon
2 tsp salt
freshly ground black pepper
2 garlic cloves
1 tbsp vinegar
1/4 tsp chopped fresh thyme
25 g/1 oz butter or margarine
2 tsp brown sugar
oil for frying
100 g/4 oz cashew nuts
100 g/4 oz mushrooms, sliced
3 onions, chopped
6 slices fresh root ginger
1 tbsp plain flour

~ Wash the chicken in cold running water, rubbing with the lemon. Season with the salt, pepper, 1 of the cloves of garlic, crushed, the vinegar and thyme. Leave to marinate for 3 hours.

~ In a large saucepan, melt the butter or margarine, then add the sugar. When it is bubbling, add the chicken and brown the pieces.

~ Meanwhile, in a frying pan, heat some oil. Fry half the cashews, then set them aside. In the same pan, fry together the remaining clove of garlic, crushed, the mushrooms, the other half of the cashews, onions and ginger. Add 50 ml/2 fl oz water and pour the mixture into the large saucepan over the chicken. Cook for 25 minutes or until the chicken is cooked.

~ Thicken with the flour mixed with some warm water and stirred into the chicken mixture. Cook for 3 more minutes, then sprinkle with the remaining fried cashews.

~ Serve with boiled rice.

Right *Calypso Chicken.*

Dominican Republic

Marinated Fried Chicken

Puerto Rico

Chicken and Rice Stew

SERVES 4

3 tbsp dark rum
3 tbsp soy sauce
3 tbsp lime juice
1.75 kg/4 lb chicken, cut into 16 pieces
1 garlic clove, crushed
½ tsp salt
freshly ground black pepper
100 g/4 oz plain flour
vegetable oil for deep frying

~Warm the rum in a small pan over a low heat. Remove the pan from the heat and set light to the rum with a match. Shake the pan backwards and forwards until the flame dies. Add the soy sauce and lime juice to the rum. Put the chicken pieces in a bowl and pour the rum mixture over them. Add the garlic, mix it in well, then leave to marinate for 4 hours, turning the pieces now and then.

~Preheat the oven to its lowest temperature and line a heatproof dish with kitchen foil.

~Heat some oil in a big frying pan. Pat the chicken pieces dry with kitchen paper and then season with the salt and freshly ground black pepper. Dip the pieces in the flour, shaking them to remove any excess, and then fry them. When the pieces are golden brown, transfer them to the prepared dish and keep them warm in the oven.

~Serve with hot boiled rice and a mixed vegetable stew.

SERVES 6

1 garlic clove, chopped
½ tsp dried oregano
½ tsp salt
1.5 kg/3 lb chicken, cut into 8 pieces
50 g/2 oz butter or margarine
1 small onion, finely chopped
75 g/3 oz green peppers, chopped
4 ripe tomatoes, skinned and chopped
350 g/12 oz uncooked long-grain white rice
1.75 l/3 pt chicken stock
freshly ground black pepper
275 g/10 oz frozen peas
50 g/2 oz Parmesan cheese, freshly grated
1 fresh hot pepper, chopped (see page 16)

~Mix the garlic, oregano and salt together in a large bowl. Add the chicken pieces and mix them well together. Heat the butter or margarine in a saucepan and brown the chicken pieces. Transfer them to a plate.

~Add the onion and green peppers to the pan and cook until soft.

~Add the tomatoes and browned chicken pieces, coating them well with the onion, peppers and tomato mixture. Reduce the heat and simmer for 30 minutes or until the chicken is cooked.

~Remove the chicken to a plate and leave to cool a little.

~Remove the bones and cut the flesh into 5-cm/2-in pieces.

~Meanwhile, add the rice, stock and freshly ground black pepper to the onion, peppers and tomato mixture and bring to the boil. Reduce the heat, cover and simmer for 20 minutes or until the rice is cooked.

~Stir in the peas, Parmesan and hot pepper. Mix well, then add the chicken. Cover and simmer for 2 more minutes, then serve.

Haiti

Poulet Roti à la Créole

Roast Chicken Creole-style

SERVES 6

100 g/4 oz butter or margarine
1 small clove garlic, peeled
25 g/1 oz soft, fresh breadcrumbs
3 tbsp lime juice
2 tsp finely grated lime rind
4 tbsp dark rum
1 tsp brown sugar
¼ tsp ground cinnamon
¼ tsp cayenne pepper
1 tsp salt
freshly ground black pepper
3 ripe bananas
1.75 kg/4 lb whole roasting chicken, turkey or goose
300 ml/10 fl oz chicken stock

48

~ Preheat oven to 180°C/350°F/Gas Mark 4.

~ Melt half the butter or margarine in a small frying pan, then add the garlic and stir it round the pan for 10 seconds. Remove and discard the garlic. Add the breadcrumbs, two-thirds of the lime juice, the lime rind, a quarter of the rum, the sugar, cinnamon, cayenne pepper, salt and freshly ground black pepper to taste. Mix well and set the stuffing on one side.

~ Peel and chop the bananas, then put them in a bowl. Add the remaining lime juice, 2 tbsp rum and salt and freshly ground black pepper to taste. Mix well together. Stuff the chicken or other fowl with the banana stuffing and sew the opening closed with a large needle and trussing string.

~ Fill the small neck cavity with the breadcrumb stuffing and sew up the opening in the same way as before.

~ Brush the chicken with the remaining butter or margarine. Place it in a roasting tin and roast in the preheated oven for 1 hour, basting occasionally with the juices.

~ After removing the chicken from the oven, transfer it to a large heated dish and leave it to rest for 5 minutes as this makes it easier to carve. Meanwhile, skim the fat from the juices left in the roasting tin and pour in the chicken stock. Bring to the boil over a high heat, stirring all the time. Cook for 2 minutes, taste for seasoning and pour into a sauceboat.

~ Just before serving, warm the last tablespoon of rum in a small pan. Remove it from the heat, then set light to the rum with a match and pour it, flaming, over the chicken and serve immediately.

Trinidad

Coriander Chicken

SERVES 4

1.5 kg/3 lb chicken, cut into 5 cm/2 in pieces
1 tsp salt
½ tsp freshly ground black pepper
3 garlic cloves
2 tsp lemon juice
2 tbsp ground coriander
1 small bunch fresh coriander
40 g/1½ oz butter or margarine

~Season the chicken with the salt, pepper, garlic, lemon juice and half the ground coriander. Chop the fresh coriander finely and mix it in with the chicken, then leave to marinate for 4 hours.

~Preheat the oven to 180°C/350°F/Gas Mark 4.

~Drain the chicken. Melt the butter or margarine. Place the chicken in a heatproof dish and pour the melted butter or margarine over the chicken. Sprinkle the remaining ground coriander over, then bake in the preheated oven for 1 hour or until the chicken is cooked.

~Just before serving, grill the chicken to brown it.

~Serve with rice and salad.

Guyana

Chicken and Noodle Bake

SERVES 4

6 chicken legs
1 tsp salt
freshly ground black pepper
1 garlic clove, crushed
25 g/1 oz butter or margarine
1 onion, chopped
1 × 295-g/10-oz tin condensed cream of mushroom soup
120 ml/4 fl oz milk
225 g/8 oz dried noodles
100 g/4 oz cheese, grated
1 tbsp chopped fresh parsley

~Season the chicken legs with the salt, pepper and garlic. Leave them to marinate for 4 hours.

~Melt the butter or margarine in a large saucepan. Add the onion and cook until soft.

~Drain the chicken legs, add them to the pan and brown them on all sides. Stir in the mushroom soup and milk, cover and simmer for 30 minutes.

~Preheat the oven to 200°C/400°F/Gas Mark 6.

~Cook the noodles as given in the instructions on the packet, then drain them and rinse in cold water. Place them in a greased heatproof dish. Arrange the chicken legs on top of the noodles, pour the sauce over and sprinkle with the cheese and parsley. Bake in the preheated oven for 30 minutes.

51

Left Coriander Chicken.

Sweet and Spicy Chicken

Poulet au Jardinière

Chicken Casserole

52

SERVES 6

1.5 kg/3 lb chicken, cut into 5 cm/2 in pieces
2 tbsp olive oil
1 onion, finely chopped
2 spring onions, finely chopped
2 garlic cloves, crushed
1 fresh hot pepper, chopped (see page 16)
1/2 tsp brown sugar
1 tsp thyme
1 tsp basil
1 christophene, peeled, deseeded and chopped
1 aubergine, peeled and cubed
100 g/4 oz okra, trimmed and chopped
400 g/14 oz tin tomatoes, drained and chopped
salt and freshly ground black pepper

~ Wash the chicken pieces.

~ Heat the oil in a large saucepan and add the onion, spring onions and garlic. Cook over a low heat for 5 minutes.

~ Add the chicken pieces and cook for 5 minutes to brown them.

~ Stir in the hot pepper, sugar, herbs and vegetables and season to taste with salt and freshly ground black pepper. Pour in 300 ml/1/2 pt of cold water and bring to the boil, then lower the heat and, stirring occasionally, simmer uncovered for 1 hour or until the chicken and vegetables are cooked and the sauce has thickened.

~ Serve with fresh bread, baked yams or boiled rice.

SERVES 6

1.5 kg/3 lb chicken, cut into 5 cm/2 in pieces
1 tsp salt
1 tsp freshly ground black pepper
2 garlic cloves
1/4 tsp chopped fresh thyme
2 tsp vinegar
1 bay leaf
2 tbsp vegetable oil
150 g/5 oz tomatoes, chopped
1 onion, finely chopped
2 celery sticks, chopped
2 carrots, diced
1/4 cabbage, shredded
4 potatoes, chopped
170 g/6 oz green beans, cleaned

~ Wash the chicken. Marinate the pieces in a bowl with the salt, pepper, garlic, thyme, bay leaf and vinegar for 5 hours.

~ Heat the oil in a large saucepan, then add the tomatoes and chicken pieces. Cover with cold water, bring it to the boil, then lower the heat and simmer, covered, for 30 minutes or until the chicken is almost cooked and the liquid has reduced.

~ Add the onion and the other vegetables and cook until they are tender but crisp.

~ Serve immediately with fresh bread or boiled rice and hot pepper sauce.

Meat Dishes

ROAST PORK CALYPSO ~ Jamaica

BAKED PAPAYA WITH MEAT FILLING ~ Jamaica

PEPPERPOT ~ Guyana

CURRIED MEATBALLS ~ Surinam

RABBIT IN PIMENTO SAUCE ~ Puerto Rico

BEEF STEAKS À L'OIGNON ~ Guadeloupe

BRAISED LAMB ~ Puerto Rico

LAMB AND SALT BEEF STEW ~ Curaçao

MINCED BEEF SPECIAL ~ Barbados

BEEF WITH BEANSPROUTS ~ Trinidad

Roast Pork Calypso

SERVES 6

1.75 kg/4 lb piece of pork
475 ml/16 fl oz cold water
1 tbsp vinegar
1 tbsp salt
3 garlic cloves, crushed
1 tsp thyme
1 onion, grated
1 tsp ground cloves
1 tbsp chopped fresh parsley

~Place the pork in a large saucepan, cover with the cold water and add the vinegar, salt, garlic and thyme. Leave to marinate for several hours.

~Meanwhile, mix the onion, cloves and parsley in a bowl.

~Preheat the oven to 325°C/160°F/Gas Mark 3.

~When the pork is ready, remove it from the saucepan and make 5-cm/2-in long gashes all over. Fill the holes with the onion mixture. Pour the marinade into a baking dish. Lay the pork in the dish and roast in the preheated oven for 30 minutes until it is done.

Baked Papaya with Meat Filling

SERVES 6

2 tbsp vegetable oil
1 small onion, finely chopped
1 garlic clove, crushed
450 g/1 lb lean minced beef or lamb
4 ripe tomatoes, skinned and chopped
2 chillies for a hot dish or ½ thinly chopped fresh hot pepper for a mild flavour
1 tsp salt
freshly ground black pepper
2.25 kg/5 lb green papaya, halved and deseeded
25 g/1 oz cheese, grated

~Preheat the oven to 180°C/350°F/Gas Mark 4.

~Heat the oil in a large frying pan and fry the onion and garlic in it for 5 minutes. Then, stir in the beef or lamb and cook until browned.

~Add the tomatoes, hot pepper, salt and freshly ground black pepper to taste. Continue to cook until all the liquid has evaporated.

~Spoon the meat mixture into the papaya shells and place them in a shallow roasting tin. Pour in enough boiling water around them to come about 2.5 cm/1 in up the sides of the shells when they are placed side by side. Bake in the preheated oven for 1 hour.

~Sprinkle with half the grated cheese and bake for another 30 minutes.

~Serve sprinkled with the remaining grated cheese.

57

Left Roast Pork Calypso.

Guyana

Pepperpot

SERVES 6

50 ml/2 fl oz vegetable oil
1.5 kg/3 lb fresh, lean pork, chopped
450 g/1 lb salt pork, chopped
900 ml/1½ pt cold water
450 g/1 lb onions, chopped
1 bunch thyme, chopped
3 garlic cloves, crushed
2 tbsp brown sugar
120 ml/4 fl oz cassareep (see page 15)
4 hot peppers

~ Heat the oil in a large saucepan and fry the meat. Cover with the cold water, then add the onions, thyme, garlic, sugar and cassareep. Tie the chillies in a clean cloth and set aside. Simmer the meat, covered, for 4 hours until it is cooked. Add the cloth containing the hot peppers and simmer for 15 minutes. Remove the pan from the heat and serve hot.

~ Pepper pot can be kept at room temperature for 3 days – the chillies and spices act as preservatives – and reheated when necessary.

58

Surinam

Curried Meatballs

MAKES 12

15 g/¹/₂ oz butter or margarine
1 onion, chopped
450 g/1 lb lean minced beef
2 tsp salt
1 tsp lemon juice
1 tsp chilli powder
1 tsp ground coriander
1 tbsp vegetable oil
150 g/5 oz onions, grated
1 garlic clove, crushed
pinch ground cloves
1 tsp turmeric
1 tsp sugar
4 tomatoes, chopped

~Melt the butter or margarine in a medium-sized saucepan and add the chopped onion. Fry it for 1-2 minutes, then add the beef, salt, lemon juice, chilli powder and coriander. Remove the pan from the heat and shape the beef mixture into balls.

~Heat the oil in the saucepan and add the grated onion, garlic, cloves, turmeric, sugar and tomatoes. Simmer for 15 minutes.

~Add the meatballs and cook for 15 more minutes.

~Serve hot with steamed rice.

59

Rabbit in Pimento Sauce

SERVES 4

850 g/2 lb rabbit, chopped into 5 cm/2 in pieces
1 tsp salt
freshly ground black pepper
50 g/2 oz butter or margarine
100 g/4 oz onions, chopped
1 fat garlic clove, chopped
2 tbsp brandy
2 tbsp sherry
3 ripe tomatoes, skinned and chopped
½ fresh hot pepper, chopped (see page 16)
50 g/2 oz drained pimentos, finely chopped
150 ml/5 fl oz chicken stock
1 bay leaf
½ tsp sugar

~Preheat the oven to 180°C/350°F/Gas Mark 4.

~Season the rabbit pieces with the salt and freshly ground black pepper to taste. Heat the butter or margarine in a large casserole and brown the rabbit. Transfer the rabbit to a dish and put to one side.

~Add the onions and garlic to the casserole, cook them for 5 minutes then pour them over the rabbit.

~Pour the brandy into the casserole and heat it. Remove the casserole from the heat and set light to the brandy with a match. Shake the casserole backwards and forwards until the flame dies. Add the sherry to the brandy in

the casserole and bring to the boil. Add the tomatoes, hot pepper, pimentos, chicken stock, bay leaf and sugar and season to taste with freshly ground black pepper. Add the rabbit, bring to the boil and cook for 30 minutes.

~Remove the casserole from the heat, cover and bake in the preheated oven for 2 hours.

~Serve with rice.

61

Beef Steaks à l'Oignon

Steaks with Onions

SERVES 6

6 very thin beef steaks
2 garlic cloves, crushed
2 tsp salt
freshly ground black pepper
1 tsp vinegar
50 g/2 oz butter or margarine
1 onion, sliced
2 tsp brandy

~Season the steaks with the garlic, salt, pepper and vinegar, then leave them to stand for 3 hours.

~In a large frying pan, heat the butter or margarine. Fry the steaks quickly to brown them on both sides, then remove them to a warm plate.

~Add the onion to the frying pan and fry for 2 minutes.

~Add the brandy to the pan, heat through, then pour the onion and brandy over the steaks and serve immediately.

~Serve with a green salad and baked sweet potatoes.

Left Rabbit in Pimento Sauce.

Puerto Rico

Braised Lamb

SERVES 6

6 lamb chops
3 tbsp honey
2 tbsp dry sherry
50 ml/2 fl oz soy sauce
2 tbsp white vinegar
2 garlic cloves, crushed
50 ml/2 fl oz chicken stock
2 tsp brown sugar
2 tbsp dark rum

~ Place the lamb chops in a glass bowl. Mix all the remaining ingredients together and pour over the chops. Refrigerate overnight.

~ Put the chops and marinade in an ovenproof dish and cover with foil or a lid. Bake in a preheated 180°C/350°F/Gas Mark 4 oven for 45 minutes, then serve at once.

~ Serve with baked cassava or breadfruit.

Curaçao

Lamb and Salt Beef Stew

SERVES 6

225 g/8 oz lean salt beef
50 g/2 oz butter or margarine
1 tbsp vegetable oil
850 g/2 lb boned lamb or goat cut into 2.5 cm/1 in pieces
225 g/8 oz onions, finely chopped
1 large tomato, skinned and chopped
2 tsp peeled and chopped fresh root ginger
25 g/1 oz green pepper, chopped
1 fat garlic clove, chopped
1/2 fresh hot pepper, chopped (see page 16)
1 tsp salt
2 tsp ground cumin
2 tbsp lime or lemon juice
600 ml/1 pt water
3 potatoes, peeled and diced
2 cucumbers, peeled and diced

~ Put the salt beef in a saucepan, cover with cold water, bring to the boil and boil for 30 minutes.

~ Drain the meat and cut it into cubes.

~ Heat the butter or margarine and oil in a large saucepan, then add the lamb or goat and brown it all over. Remove the meat and set to one side.

~ Add the onions to the saucepan and cook for 5 minutes. Then add the tomato, ginger, green pepper, garlic, hot pepper, salt and cumin. Cook for 10 minutes, stirring all the time.

~ Stir in the prepared salt beef, lamb, lime or lemon juice and 600 ml/1 pt of water. Cook for 1 hour over low heat.

~ Add the potatoes and cucumber and simmer for 20 more minutes.

Minced Beef Special

SERVES 6

850 g/2 lb minced beef
1 tsp salt
freshly ground black pepper
½ tsp thyme
2 spring onions, chopped
450 g/1 lb chestnuts
50 ml/2 fl oz olive oil
1 large onion, chopped
2 garlic cloves, crushed
900 ml/1½ pt water
1 tsp chopped fresh basil
750 g/1½ lb rice
50 g/2 oz cashew nuts, chopped

~Season the minced beef with the salt, pepper, thyme and spring onions and leave to infuse for 1 hour.

~Cook the chestnuts in boiling water until they are soft and shell them once they are cool enough to handle.

~In a saucepan, heat the oil, then add the onion and garlic and cook for 5 minutes over a medium heat. Add the minced beef and cook until it has lightly browned all over. Add 900 ml/1½ pt of cold water and the basil and simmer.

~Meanwhile, wash the rice and drain it well. Add the rice to the beef mixture and cook until the rice is tender and the water has been absorbed. Sprinkle over the cashews.

~Serve hot with a green salad.

64

***Above** Coconut palms, Trinidad.*

Beef with Beansprouts

SERVES 4

450 g/1 lb lean beef, cut into tiny pieces
½ tsp salt
freshly ground black pepper
1 garlic clove, crushed
1 tbsp vegetable oil
1 tbsp soy sauce
150 g/5 oz onions, chopped
2 tbsp beef stock
50 g/2 oz fresh beansprouts

~Season the beef with the salt, freshly ground black pepper to taste and the garlic.

~Heat the oil in a frying pan, then add the soy sauce. Fry the beef until it is evenly browned, then add the onions and stock. Cook for 5 minutes, stirring all the time, then lower the heat, add the beansprouts and cook for 10 more minutes.

~Serve with steamed rice and hot pepper sauce.

***Right** Beef with Beansprouts.*

Fish and Seafood Dishes

BAKED LOBSTER ~ Jamaica

LOBSTER IN CHILLI SAUCE ~ Cuba

BLAFF ~ Martinique

FRIED FLYING FISH ~ Barbados

COURT BOUILLON À LA CRÉOLE ~ Martinique

RICE WITH PRAWNS AND TOMATOES ~ Dominica

BAKED EDAM CHEESE WITH PRAWN STUFFING ~ Curaçao

CRABS IN PEPPER SAUCE ~ Dominican Republic

CRAB GUMBO ~ Antigua

BAKED FISH WITH ONIONS ~ Cuba

Fish Tips

The Caribbean waters are rich in fish and seafood. Typical Caribbean fish are grouper, kingfish, Spanish mackerel, snappers, flying fish (a fish with "wings" that are, in fact, extended fins, found off the coasts of Barbados) and dolphin fish – no relation to the mammal.

~Some Caribbean fish have bizarre shapes: the coffer fish is square-shaped and the moonfish is round and silvery, for example. The people of Martinique have named a fish "bon-die marie moin", which is Creole meaning "good God handled me", for this fish has unearthly fingerprints along its sides.

~The Caribbean waters also contain plenty of crabs, prawns, octopus, spiny lobsters, conch (called lambi), which are enormous sea snails with big horns, and sea eggs (a kind of white sea urchin without spines).

~When you buy fish, make sure that it is fresh. Signs of this are eyes that are clear and bright (avoid those with sunken eyes), skin that is shiny and moist, flesh that is firm and a sea-fresh smell. Frozen fish should be frozen hard with no sign of partial thawing.

~When buying shellfish, make sure the shells are undamaged, with no cracks.

~Most fishmongers will clean, bone and fillet fish for you. Nowadays many exotic fish are on display at fishmongers and in supermarkets, including mackerel, jacks or trevally, kingfish, snapper, swordfish, tuna, sea bream, parrotfish and pomfrets. Octopus, squid, prawns, crabs and lobster are also available.

Jamaica

Baked Lobster

SERVES 4

850 g/2 lb cooked lobster meat, cubed
2 tsp salt
1 garlic clove, crushed
1/4 tsp nutmeg
freshly ground black pepper
50 g/2 oz butter or margarine
900 ml/1 1/2 pt single cream or evaporated milk
1 tsp hot pepper sauce
1/2 small onion, finely chopped
2 egg yolks
100 g/4 oz cheese, grated

~Put the lobster into a bowl and stir in the salt, garlic, nutmeg and freshly ground black pepper. Chill it for 1 hour.

~Preheat the oven to 180°C/350°F/Gas Mark 4.

~Melt the butter or margarine in a large saucepan over a low heat. Gradually add the cream or evaporated milk, stirring all the time. Add the lobster, hot pepper sauce and onion, mixing them in well. Beat the egg yolks slightly, then add them to the saucepan.

~Spoon the lobster mixture into a greased baking dish. Sprinkle half the grated cheese over and bake in the preheated oven for 5 minutes.

~Sprinkle the remaining cheese over just before serving.

~Serve on a bed of rice or with mashed sweet potatoes.

Cuba

Lobster in Chilli Sauce

SERVES 2

2 × 850 g/2 lb uncooked lobsters, split in half lengthways
2 tbsp vegetable oil mixed with 1 tsp liquid annatto (see page 14)
300 ml/10 fl oz dry white wine
1 tsp salt
1/2 hot pepper, finely chopped (see page 16)

~Remove and discard the gelatinous sac in the head of each lobster and the long intestinal vein attached to it. Chop off the tail section of each lobster at the point where it joins the body. Twist off the claws and smash the flat side of each claw with a large, heavy knife. Cut off and discard the small claws and antennae.

~Heat the oil in a large frying pan. Add the lobster bodies, tails and large claws and fry them, stirring constantly, until the shells turn pink. Transfer the lobsters to a large plate.

~Add the wine to the frying pan and bring it to the boil. Stir in the salt and hot pepper. Return the lobsters to the pan, coat them evenly in the liquid and cook for 10 minutes, basting them from time to time.

~To serve, arrange the lobster pieces in a large, heated dish and spoon the sauce over them.

***Right** Lobster in Chilli Sauce.*

Martinique

Blaff

Poached Marinated Fish

SERVES 2

1.2 l/2 pt water
6 tbsp fresh lime or lemon juice
2 tsp salt
2 × 450 g/1 lb fish, scaled, cleaned and cut into four fish
steaks about 2.5 cm/1 in thick (snapper, sea bream,
jack or mullet)
1 small onion, finely chopped
1 tsp crushed garlic cloves
1 hot pepper, chopped (see page 16)
2 bay leaves
1/2 tsp thyme

~ Put half the water, half the lime or lemon juice and salt into a large, shallow, glass baking dish. Wash the fish steaks under cold running water, then put them in the baking dish and leave to marinate for about 1 hour.

~ Drain and discard the marinade.

~ Pour the remaining water into a frying pan, together with the onion, garlic, hot pepper, bay leaves and thyme. Bring to the boil over a high heat, then lower the heat and simmer for 5 minutes.

~ Add the fish steaks to the pan and bring back to the boil. Reduce the heat to the lowest setting, cover the pan and simmer for 10 minutes or until the fish is cooked. Transfer the fish to a warmed serving dish. Add the remaining lime or lemon juice to the cooking liquid and pour this over the fish. Taste to check the seasoning, then serve at once.

~ Serve with fresh bread.

Barbados

Fried Flying Fish

SERVES 6

6 small, boned flying fish
1 tbsp lime or lemon juice
1 garlic clove, crushed
salt and freshly ground black pepper
1 tsp chopped fresh thyme
2 whole cloves
2 tsp plain flour
vegetable oil for frying

~ Marinate the fish in the lemon or lime juice, garlic, salt and freshly ground black pepper, thyme and cloves for at least 1 hour.

~ Remove the fish from the marinade and dry it well with kitchen towel.

~ Mix the flour with freshly ground black pepper then coat the fish in it, shaking off any excess.

~ Heat some oil (enough to cover the fish) in a big frying pan. Fry the fish until they are golden brown, then serve.

~ Serve hot with rice and peas, salad and hot pepper sauce.

71

Left Blaff.

Martinique

Court Bouillon à la Créole

Braised Marinated Fish Creole Style

SERVES 4

600 ml/1 pt water
6 tbsp fresh lime or lemon juice
2 tsp salt
850 g/2 lb firm fish (such as snapper or mullet), scaled,
cleaned and cut into 4 × 225 g/8 oz steaks
3 tbsp vegetable oil mixed with 1 tsp liquid annatto
(see page 14)
100 g/4 oz spring onions, chopped
4 garlic cloves, chopped
½ hot pepper, finely chopped (see page 16)
3 ripe tomatoes, skinned and chopped
1 tsp thyme
1 bay leaf
4 parsley sprigs
freshly ground black pepper
2 tbsp olive oil

72

~ Put 450 ml/¾ pt water, the lime or lemon juice and salt into a large, shallow, glass dish and stir until the salt dissolves. Wash the fish steaks under cold running water and marinate them in the lime or lemon juice mixture for 1 hour.

~ Remove the fish from the marinade. Heat the annatto-flavoured oil in a large saucepan over a medium heat. Add the spring onions, garlic and hot pepper and cook until soft.

~ Add the tomatoes, thyme, bay leaf, parsley and freshly ground black pepper and simmer for 10 minutes.

~ Stir in the remaining water, add the fish and bring to the boil. Reduce the heat and simmer for 10 more minutes.

~ Transfer the fish and sauce to a heated baking dish. Sprinkle over the olive oil and bake in the preheated oven for 5 minutes.

Above *Codfish – salted cod is a Caribbean speciality.*

Dominica

Rice with Prawns and Tomatoes

SERVES 4

2 tbsp olive oil
1 garlic clove, crushed
2 tomatoes, peeled and chopped
1 tsp saffron
2 tsp salt
1 tsp paprika
225 g/8 oz peas
350g/12 oz uncooked rice
freshly ground black pepper
600 ml/1 pt water
8 prawns, cooked, shelled and deveined
12 scampi, cooked, shelled and deveined

~ Heat the oil in a saucepan, then fry the garlic in it for 2 minutes.

~ Add the tomatoes, saffron, salt, paprika, peas, rice and freshly ground black pepper and fry for 5 minutes, then add the water.

~ Add the prawns and scampi and cook for 15 more minutes or until the rice has cooked (if necessary adding some more water). Serve immediately.

~ Serve with a cucumber salad.

Left *Rice with Prawns and Tomatoes.*

Curaçao

Baked Edam Cheese with Prawn Stuffing

SERVES 6

1.75 kg/4 lb whole Edam cheese
50 g/2 oz butter or margarine
2 tsp vegetable oil
¹/₂ oz onion, finely chopped
1 tomato, skinned and chopped
¹/₄ tsp chilli powder
¹/₂ tsp salt
freshly ground black pepper
350 g/12 oz cooked prawns, shelled, deveined and chopped
3 tbsp soft, fresh, white breadcrumbs
1 egg, well beaten
2 tbsp raisins

~ Peel the wax off the cheese and cut a 2.5-cm/1-in thick slice off the top and reserve. Scoop out the centre of the cheese with a spoon to leave a shell 2.5 cm/1 in thick, reserving the scooped out cheese.

~ Place the shell and top in enough cold water to cover them and leave them to soak for 1 hour.

~ Remove the cheese shell and top from the water, turn them upside down and leave them on kitchen paper to drain.

~ Grate the cheese removed from the centre.

~ Preheat the oven to 180°C/350°F/Gas Mark 4.

~ Grease a round baking dish with half the butter or margarine (it has to be large enough to hold the cheese shell – not too shallow or too large but about the same size as the cheese shell).

~ Heat the remaining butter or margarine and vegetable oil in a frying pan over a medium heat. Add the onion and cook for 5 minutes, not letting it catch.

~ Add the tomato, chilli powder, salt and a few grindings of black pepper. Continue to cook until the mixture becomes thick, then transfer it to a bowl. Add the grated cheese, prawns, breadcrumbs, egg and raisins. Spoon the mixture into the cheese shell and cover with the cheese top and put it in the prepared baking dish. Bake it in the preheated oven, uncovered, for 30 minutes until the top has browned slightly.

~ Serve at once, straight from the baking dish.

75

Dominican Republic

Crabs in Pepper Sauce

SERVES 6

3 tbsp olive oil
1 hot pepper, finely chopped
1 medium onion, finely chopped
1/2 green pepper, finely chopped
2 garlic cloves, finely chopped
6 ripe tomatoes, skinned and chopped
3 tbsp tomato purée
1 tsp salt
freshly ground black pepper
450 g/1 lb fresh, tinned or frozen crabmeat
2 tbsp fresh lime or lemon juice
2 tbsp finely chopped fresh coriander

~Heat the oil in a large frying pan over a medium heat. Add the hot pepper, onion, green pepper and garlic and fry for 5 minutes.

~Add the tomatoes, tomato purée, salt and freshly ground black pepper to taste. Bring the mixture to the boil, then lower the heat and cook, uncovered, until it has reduced to a thick sauce.

~Add the crabmeat and stir it in. Simmer for 2 minutes.

~Serve sprinkled with the lime or lemon juice and chopped coriander.

Antigua

Crab Gumbo

SERVES 6

2 × 850 g/2 lb cooked crabs
25 g/1 oz butter or margarine
1 tbsp vegetable oil
1 onion, chopped
400 g/14 oz tin tomatoes, drained and chopped
1 tbsp chopped fresh thyme
2 tbsp chopped fresh parsley
225 g/8 oz okra, trimmed and sliced
1 fresh hot pepper
600 ml/1 pt boiling water
salt and freshly ground black pepper

~Cut the legs and claws off the crabs and crack them using a nutcracker. Cut the body into quarters.

~Heat the butter or margarine and oil in a large saucepan over a medium heat. Add the onion and fry for 5 minutes.

~Add the crabs and cook, turning the pieces over frequently.

~Stir in the tomatoes, thyme and parsley and cook for 5 more minutes.

~Add the okra and chilli and pour in 600 ml/ 1 pt boiling water. Season with salt and freshly ground black pepper, then lower the heat and simmer for 45 minutes.

~Discard the hot pepper and spoon the stew into warmed soup bowls.

~Serve with fresh bread.

Right *Crab Gumbo.*

Cuba

Baked Fish with Onions

SERVES 6

850 g/2 lb red snappers or similar fish
salt and freshly ground black pepper
2 garlic cloves, crushed
juice of 1 lemon
250 ml/8 fl oz water
1 large onion, finely chopped
25 g/1 oz fresh breadcrumbs
120 ml/4 fl oz olive oil
1 tbsp chopped fresh parsley

~Clean, wash and prepare the fish. Make an incision along the belly of each fish. Lightly sprinkle salt and freshly ground black pepper and some garlic both inside and outside. Rub lemon juice over the fish. If possible leave the fish to marinate for 4 hours, but at least 1 hour, in the water.

~Preheat the oven to 180°C/350°F/Gas Mark 4.

~Cook half the onion, the remaining garlic and half the breadcrumbs in 1 tablespoon of the oil. Add a little water to make the mixture form a slightly crumbly texture and leave it to cool.

~Stuff the fish with the onion and breadcrumbs mixture, then lay them in a greased baking dish and cover with the rest of the oil. Sprinkle the rest of the onion and breadcrumbs and the parsley over them. Bake them in the preheated oven for 30 minutes.

78

Vegetables and Pulses

GREEN PLANTAIN CHIPS ~ Jamaica

STEWED OKRAS ~ Puerto Rico

PIONONOS ~ Puerto Rico

BLACK BEANS AND RICE ~ Cuba

AUBERGINES IN COCONUT SAUCE ~ Martinique

SWEET POTATO AND WALNUT SOUFFLÉ ~ Antigua

YAM SOUFFLÉ ~ Barbados

ACKEE AND SALT FISH ~ Jamaica

JUG JUG ~ Barbados

BAKED CHRISTOPHENE ~ Martinique

Jamaica

Green Plantain Chips

Stewed Okra

SERVES 6

4 green plantains
juice of ½ lime
salt
vegetable oil for deep frying

~ Peel the plantains (see page 17) and rub them with the lime juice. Cut them into thin slices and mix well with a pinch of salt.

~ Heat some oil in a large frying pan. Drain the plantain slices, then fry them for 3 minutes until they are crisp and golden brown.

~ Remove them from the pan as they are ready and drain them on kitchen paper.

~ Serve when cool.

SERVES 6

850 g/2 lb fresh okra
25 g/1 oz butter or margarine
175 g/6 oz onions, finely chopped
1 garlic clove, crushed
8 ripe tomatoes, skinned and chopped
½ hot pepper, chopped (see page 16)
1 tsp salt

~ Wash the okra under cold running water. Cut 1 cm/½ in off the stalk, at the narrow end.

~ Melt the butter or margarine in a large saucepan over a medium heat. Add the onions and garlic and fry until they are soft.

~ Add the tomatoes and hot pepper and cook for 5 more minutes.

~ Add the okra and salt, stir, then reduce the heat. Cook for 20 more minutes or until the okra are soft.

~ Serve with rice and fried fish.

Piononos

Deep-fried Plantain Rings with Minced Beef

SERVES 4

2 big, ripe plantains
50 g/2 oz butter or margarine
2 tsp vegetable oil
2 tbsp vegetable oil mixed with 1 tsp liquid annatto
450 g/1 lb lean minced beef
1 small onion, chopped
½ green pepper, chopped
1 fresh hot pepper, chopped
1 garlic clove, crushed
15 g/½ oz plain flour
3 ripe tomatoes, skinned and chopped
3 tbsp water
1 tsp salt
freshly ground black pepper
1½ tbsp vinegar
4 eggs
vegetable oil for frying

~ Peel the plantains (see page 17).

~ Heat the butter or margarine with the vegetable oil in a large frying pan. Cut each plantain lengthways into 4 thick slices. Cook them in the pan for 4 minutes, turning them over now and again until they have browned. Drain them on kitchen paper.

~ Heat the annatto-flavoured oil in the same pan over a medium heat and add the beef, onion, green pepPer, hot pepper and garlic. Cook for 5 minutes.

~ Add the flour and stir it in, then add the tomatoes, water, salt and freshly ground black pepper to taste. Cook until the mixture thickens.

~ Stir in the vinegar.

~ To make piononos, carefully bend each plantain slice round into a ring about 7.5 cm/3 in in diameter, securing the overlapping ends with a wooden cocktail stick. Lay the rings side by side.

~ Spoon the beef mixture into each ring and press the tops as flat as possible.

~ Beat the eggs and brush some over the piononos.

~ Heat enough oil in a large pan to deep-fry the piononos. Fry them for about 3 minutes each side, turning them over very gently. Drain them on kitchen paper and serve as soon as they are all cooked.

~ Serve with rice 'n' peas or Black Beans and Rice (see page 86).

85

Left *Piononos served with rice and garden peas – an alternative to traditional rice 'n' peas.*

Cuba

Black Beans and Rice

SERVES 6

175 g/6 oz dried black beans
2.65 l/4¾ pt water
3 tbsp vegetable oil
1 small onion, chopped
1 garlic clove, chopped
½ green pepper, chopped
275 g/10 oz uncooked long-grain white rice
1 tsp salt
freshly ground black pepper

~Rinse the beans in a colander under cold running water until the water runs clear.

~Bring all but 450 ml/15 fl oz of the water to the boil in a large saucepan, add the beans, reduce the heat and simmer for 3 hours or until done.

~Drain the beans in a colander. Mash 2 tablespoons of the beans to a smooth paste with a fork.

~Heat the oil in a large frying pan. Add the onion, garlic and green pepper and cook them until soft.

~Stir in the bean paste and then add the rest of the beans. Reduce the heat and simmer, uncovered, for 10 minutes.

~Return the contents of the frying pan to the large saucepan. Add the rice, salt and remaining water, bring to the boil, then reduce the heat, cover and simmer for 20 minutes or until the rice is cooked.

~Season to taste with salt and freshly ground black pepper.

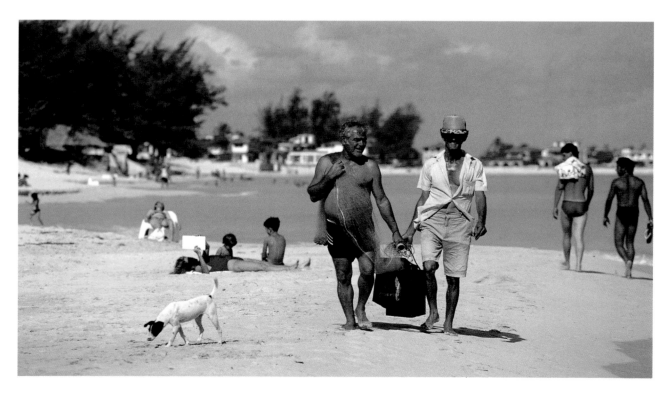

Above Fishermen on Varadero Beach, Cuba.

Martinique

Aubergines in Coconut Sauce

SERVES 6

850 g/2 lb aubergines
1 tbsp salt
8 tbsp oil
2 onions, sliced
2 garlic cloves, crushed
6 tomatoes, skinned and chopped
300 ml/1/2 pt coconut milk (see page 15)
freshly ground black pepper
2 tbsp desiccated coconut

~Cut the aubergines into 1 cm/1/2 in thick slices. Place them in a colander, sprinkling a little salt over each layer of slices, and leave, weighted down with a plate, for 20 minutes. Rinse off the bitter juices that have oozed out and dry with kitchen paper.

~Heat 6 tablespoons oil in a large frying pan. Fry the aubergine slices for 10 minutes, turning them once during this time. Drain them on kitchen paper.

~Preheat the oven to 180°C/350°F/Gas Mark 4.

~Heat the remaining oil in the same pan, add the onions and fry for 5 minutes over a medium heat.

~Add the garlic and tomatoes and cook for 3 minutes, stirring constantly.

~Pour in the coconut milk and season to taste with salt and freshly ground black pepper. Layer the aubergine slices in an ovenproof dish and pour over the coconut sauce. Cover with foil and bake in the preheated oven for 30 minutes.

~Uncover, sprinkle the desiccated coconut over and bake for 5 more minutes.

89

Antigua

Sweet Potato and Walnut Soufflé

SERVES 6

4 small sweet potatoes
25 g/1 oz butter or margarine
2 tbsp flour
250 ml/8 fl oz milk
1/2 small onion, grated
1/4 tsp thyme
freshly ground black pepper
4 eggs, separated
150 g/5 oz walnuts, chopped

~Cook the sweet potatoes in boiling water until they are soft. Drain them and leave them to cool. Peel the sweet potatoes, then mash them with a fork.

~Preheat the oven to its lowest setting.

~In a saucepan, melt the butter or margarine, then stir in the flour. Gradually add the milk, stirring, and cook until the sauce thickens.

Remove the pan from the heat and add the onion, thyme and freshly ground black pepper. Beat the egg whites until they are stiff, then gently fold them into the sauce.

~Add the walnuts and sweet potato, stirring them in gently. Beat the egg yolks and add these to the mixture. Pour the mixture into a greased soufflé dish. Bake in the preheated oven for 20 minutes, then serve immediately.

Left *Aubergines in Coconut Sauce.*

Barbados

Yam Soufflé

SERVES 4

3 small yams, peeled and quartered
50 g/2 oz butter or margarine
300 ml/¹/₂ pt milk
25 g/1 oz cheese, grated
1 tsp salt
2 eggs, separated
freshly ground black pepper

~Boil the yams until they are soft, then drain and mash them with a fork. Beat in the butter or margarine and gradually add the milk.

~Add half the cheese, the salt, egg yolks and freshly ground black pepper to taste.

~Preheat the oven to 180°C/350°F/Gas Mark 4 and grease a baking dish.

~Beat the egg whites until they are stiff and gently mix them into the yam mixture. Carefully spoon the mixture into the prepared baking dish. Sprinkle the remaining grated cheese over and bake for 30 minutes until the top has gently browned. Serve at once.

90

Jamaica

Ackee and Salt Fish

SERVES 6

850 g/2 lb salt cod
50 ml/2 fl oz vegetable oil
1 onion, sliced
1 garlic clove, crushed
1 fresh hot pepper, chopped (see page 16)
2 tomatoes, skinned and chopped
400 g/14 oz tin ackee

~Soak the cod overnight to remove the salt. Next day, drain it, then rinse it well under cold running water and break into flakes. Discard the skin and bones. Heat the oil in a frying pan, add the onion, garlic and hot pepper and fry over a low heat until they are soft.

~Add the prepared salt cod and fry for 5 minutes, stirring constantly.

~Add the tomatoes and cook for 5 more minutes.

~Add the ackee and cook until it looks like scrambled eggs, then serve.

~Serve hot with rice 'n' peas and fried plantains.

Right *Ackee and Salt Fish served with rice and garden peas.*

Jug Jug

Pigeon Peas with Salt Beef and Cornmeal

SERVES 8

225 g/8 oz lean salt beef
375 g/13 oz dried pigeon peas
225 g/8 oz lean salt pork, cut into 5 pieces
1.75 l/3 pt water
50 g/2 oz yellow cornmeal
1 tsp thyme
75 g/3 oz butter or margarine
1 medium onion, chopped
salt and freshly ground black pepper

~Put the salt beef into a heavy saucepan with enough water to cover. Bring to the boil, then reduce the heat and simmer, covered, for 3 hours.

~Drain the beef then mince it coarsely.

~Wash the pigeon peas under cold running water, then put them, the salt pork and water into a large saucepan. Bring to the boil, reduce the heat, then partially cover the pan and simmer for 2 hours.

~Drain, reserving the cooking liquid (you should have 750 ml/1¼ pt, but if it is less, make it up to this amount with cold water). Mince the pork and peas coarsely. Return the cooking liquid to the pan and bring to the boil, then pour in the cornmeal and whisk it in. Add the thyme and boil for 10 minutes until the mixture is thick.

~Melt a third of the butter or margarine in a large frying pan. Add the onion and cook for 5 minutes, stirring, until soft.

~Stir in the cornmeal-thickened sauce, pork and peas and beef. Season to taste with salt and freshly ground black pepper and simmer for 20 minutes. Stir in the remaining butter and serve at once.

***Above** Bridgetown, Barbados.*

Baked Christophene

SERVES 4

2 christophenes
250 ml/8 fl oz water
½ tsp salt
1 onion, chopped
15 g/½ oz butter or margarine
freshly ground black pepper
1 tsp breadcrumbs

~Preheat the oven to 180°C/350°F/Gas Mark 4.

~Peel the christophenes then cut them into small pieces and boil in the water, to which the salt has been added, until soft. Drain well and mash with a fork.

~Add the onion, half the butter or margarine and freshly ground black pepper.

~Grease a baking dish with the remaining butter or margarine, pour the mashed christophene into it, sprinkle with the breadcrumbs and bake in the preheated oven for 15 minutes.

***Right** Baked Christophene.*

Desserts

MANGO MOUSSE ~ Trinidad

SWEET POTATO FLAPJACKS ~ Grenada

BANANA FRITTERS ~ Martinique

PUMPKIN PIE ~ Surinam

GUAVA PIE ~ Jamaica

TROPICAL FRUIT SALAD ~ St Lucia

SOURSOP ICE-CREAM ~ Guyana

COCONUT-MILK SORBET ~ Barbados

PINEAPPLE FOOL ~ Jamaica

BAKED BANANAS FLAMBÉES ~ Antigua

Trinidad

Mango Mousse

SERVES 8

5 medium, ripe mangoes (see page 16)
3 tbsp lime or lemon juice
2 egg whites
pinch of salt
50 g/2 oz caster sugar
6 tbsp double cream

~ Dice the flesh of 2 of the mangoes and purée the rest in a blender.

~ Put the purée into a glass mixing bowl and stir in the lime or lemon juice.

~ Beat the egg whites with the salt until they are frothy. Sprinkle in the sugar and continue to beat until stiff. Gently fold in the cream. Gently stir the mixture into the mango purée. Pour over the diced mango. Spoon the mixture into serving bowls or glasses and chill for at least 3 hours before serving.

96

Grenada

Sweet Potato Flapjacks

SERVES 6

450 g/1 lb sweet potatoes
175 g/6 oz butter or margarine
1/2 tsp salt
225 g/8 oz light brown sugar
2 eggs
1/2 tsp freshly grated nutmeg
1/2 tsp ground ginger
2 tbsp rum

~ Preheat the oven to 180°C/350°F/Gas Mark 4.

~ Peel and grate the sweet potatoes.

~ Cream the butter or margarine with the salt and gradually blend in the sugar. Beat until light and fluffy.

~ Add the eggs, nutmeg, ginger, rum and grated sweet potato, mixing well. Spoon the mixture into a greased baking dish, smooth the top and bake in the preheated oven for 60 minutes.

~ Leave to cool, then cut it into slices.

~ Serve with rum-flavoured whipped cream.

Right *Sweet Potato Flapjacks.*

Martinique

Banana Fritters

SERVES 6

225 g/8 oz plain flour
pinch of salt
1 tsp baking powder
9 tbsp milk
1 egg
15 g/¹/₂ oz butter or margarine, melted
75 g/3 oz sugar
3 small, ripe bananas
3 tbsp light rum
2 tbsp lime or lemon juice
vegetable oil for frying
25 g/1 oz coconut meat or cheese, grated

~ Make a batter by putting the flour, salt, baking powder, milk, egg, melted butter or margarine and a third of the sugar in a blender and mixing it at high speed. Pour the batter into a bowl.

~ Peel the bananas and cut them into 2.5 cm/ 1 in slices. Mix them in a bowl with the rum, lime or lemon juice and half the remaining sugar. Leave them to marinate for 1 hour.

~ Heat the oil in a little frying pan until it is very hot. Drain the banana slices, dip them into the batter and fry until they are golden brown, then drain them on kitchen paper.

~ Sprinkle the grated coconut or grated cheese over them and place under a hot grill for 2 minutes. Serve hot.

99

Surinam

Pumpkin Pie

SERVES 6

450 g/1 lb pumpkin
250 ml/8 fl oz water
15 g/¹/₂ oz butter or margarine
2 eggs
150 ml/5 fl oz milk
¹/₂ tsp freshly grated nutmeg
1 tsp cinnamon
90 g/3¹/₂ oz sugar
1 × 23 cm/9 in shortcrust pastry pie case, baked blind and cooled (see page 100)

~ Peel the pumpkin and cut the flesh into cubes. Cook in the water until it is soft. Drain it and mash it with a fork.

~ Preheat the oven to 230°C/450°F/Gas Mark 8.

~ In a saucepan, melt the butter or margarine. Beat the eggs and mix in the milk, nutmeg and cinnamon. Add this mixture to the melted butter or margarine and cook over a medium heat for 15 minutes.

~ Pour in the sugar and mashed pumpkin, stir well together and cook for 10 more minutes.

~ Remove the pan from the heat and leave to cool.

~ Spoon the pumpkin filling into the pie case and bake in the preheated oven for 10 minutes, then lower the heat to 150°C/ 300°F/Gas Mark 2 and bake until firm.

Left Banana Fritters.

Guava Pie

MAKES ONE 23 cm/9 in PIE

2 × 900 g/2 lb 2 oz tins guavas
3 tbsp lime or lemon juice
2 tsp arrowroot, blended with 1½ tbsp cold water
shortcrust pastry pie case, baked blind and cooled
300 ml/½ pt chilled double cream, whipped
lime zest to decorate

~ Drain the guavas, reserving the liquid, and place them in a glass bowl on one side.

~ Pour the reserved guava liquid into an enamel saucepan and cook until it has reduced to 150 ml/5 fl oz.

~ Add the lime or lemon juice and arrowroot mixture to the boiling liquid, stirring constantly until the mixture is thick.

~ Remove the pan from the heat and, using a pastry brush, coat the inside of the pie case with a little over half of the mixture.

~ Place the guavas in the pie case, then pour the remaining guava syrup over them and leave to cool at room temperature.

~ Serve with the whipped cream and decorate with lime zest.

SHORTCRUST PASTRY

TO MAKE ONE 20-23 CM/8-9 IN PASTRY CASE

75 g/3 oz unsalted butter, chilled and cut into
0.5 cm/¼ in pieces
25 g/1 oz lard, chilled and cut into
0.5 cm/¼ in pieces
150 g/6 oz plain flour
15 g/½ oz sugar
¼ tsp salt
2–3 tbsp iced water
15 g/½ oz butter (for a "blind" case)

~ Put the butter, lard, flour, sugar and salt into a large, chilled bowl. Rub the flour and fats together with your finger-tips until they look like fine breadcrumbs. Do not let the mixture become oily.

~ Pour 2½ tablespoons of iced water over the mixture, toss it together lightly and gather it into a ball. If the dough crumbles, gradually add up to 2½ teaspoons more iced water. Dust the pastry dough with a little flour and wrap it in grease-proof paper. Refrigerate for at least an hour before using.

~ To prepare a blind, or unfilled, baked pastry case, spread 15 g/½ oz butter over the bottom and sides of a 23-cm/9-in pie tin. Pat the prepared dough into a rough circle about 2.5 cm/1 in thick on a floured surface. Dust a little flour over and under it and roll it out from the centre to within 2.5 cm/1 in of the far edge. Lift the dough and turn it clockwise about 5 cm/2 in; roll again from the centre. Repeat until the dough is 0.25 cm/⅛ in thick and 32–35 cm/13–14 in in diameter.

~ Roll the dough onto a rolling pin and unroll it slackly over the pie tin. Cut off the excess dough leaving 2.5 cm/1 in all round. Chill for 1 hour. Preheat the oven to 200°C/400°F/Gas Mark 6. Spread a sheet of buttered aluminium foil across the tin and press it gently into the edge of the case. Bake on the middle shelf for about 10 minutes then remove the foil. Prick the pastry, then return it to the oven for a further 10 minutes until it begins to brown. Remove and cool.

Tropical Fruit Salad

SERVES 6

1 fresh pineapple, peeled and sliced (see page 17), or
400 g/14 oz tin pineapple slices
3 tbsp rum
40 g/1¹/₂ oz brown sugar
juice of 1 lemon
2 bananas, sliced
2 mangoes, sliced
2 ripe guavas, sliced
5 tbsp grated fresh coconut meat
¹/₂ tsp freshly grated nutmeg

~Put the pineapple slices into a glass bowl. Add the rum and sugar and chill, covered, for 1 hour.

~Pour in the lemon juice and mix in all the fruit. Serve sprinkled with the grated coconut and nutmeg.

103

Above *Marie island cactus, St Lucia.*

Guyana

Soursop Ice-cream

SERVES 4

1 medium soursop
475 ml/16 fl oz water
2 × 400 g/14 oz tins condensed milk
300 ml/10 fl oz evaporated milk
1 tsp butter or margarine
¼ tsp vanilla essence
sugar to taste
3 tbsp cornflour

~Cut the soursop in half. Remove the flesh with a spoon and mix it with a quarter of the water. Press it through a sieve to extract the pulp.

~Mix the milks and remaining water in a saucepan and bring to the boil.

~Add the butter or margarine, vanilla essence and sugar to taste.

~Mix the cornflour with a little warm water, then add it to the mixture in the pan, stirring all the time until it thickens well. Remove the pan from the heat and leave to cool.

~Add the soursop pulp to the pan, mix it in well, then transfer to shallow freezer containers and freeze for 3 hours, beating it every 30 minutes or so to break down the ice crystals. Otherwise, follow the instructions if you have an ice-cream maker. Remove the ice-cream from the freezer at least 30 minutes before serving so it will be soft enough to serve.

Above *Kingstown market, St Vincent.*

Barbados

Coconut-milk Sorbet

MAKES 600 ml/1 pt

750 g/1½ lb fresh coconut meat (see page 15)
450 ml/15 fl oz milk, warmed
3 tbsp water
225 g/8 oz sugar
2 drops vanilla essence
fresh mint leaves to decorate

~Preheat the oven to 180°C/350°F/Gas Mark 4.

~Grate 225 g/8 oz of the coconut. Sprinkle it in a roasting tin and roast in the preheated oven for 15 minutes or until it has lightly browned. Set it to one side.

~Make coconut milk from the remaining coconut and the warm milk (see page 15).

~Bring the water and sugar to the boil in a saucepan and heat until the sugar has dissolved, then leave it to cool.

~Add the vanilla essence, coconut milk and roasted coconut to the syrup, stir well, then pour the mixture into 2 ice cube trays from which the dividers have been removed. Freeze the sorbet for 3 hours, stirring every 30 minutes to break up the large ice crystals. Sorbet should have a fine, firm texture when ready. Remove it from the freezer at least 30 minutes before serving so it will be soft enough to scoop out.

~Serve in small bowls, decorated with the mint leaves.

Jamaica

Pineapple Fool

SERVES 4

350 g/12 oz fresh pineapple, papaya or mango, finely chopped (see pages 14–17)
300 ml/10 fl oz double cream
½ tsp vanilla essence
3 tbsp icing sugar

~Drain the pineapple, papaya or mango.

~Whip the cream together with the vanilla essence and a third of the icing sugar.

~Chill the cream and pineapple, papaya or mango separately for 1 hour.

~Just before serving, fold the cream into the pineapple, papaya or mango and serve at once in small bowls.

Baked Bananas Flambées

SERVES 4

4 large, ripe bananas
3 tbsp light rum
50 g/2 oz butter or margarine
75 g/3 oz sugar
1/2 tsp ground allspice
2 tbsp fresh lime or lemon juice

~ Preheat the oven to 200°C/400°F/Gas Mark 6.

~ Pierce the unpeeled bananas with a fork, place on a baking sheet and bake in the preheated oven for 10-15 minutes or until soft.

~ Leave them to cool, then peel off the skins.

~ Warm the rum in a small frying pan.

~ In another pan, melt the butter or margarine, then add the sugar and allspice and mix well. Coat the bananas in this mixture and put each one in a serving dish. Sprinkle the lime or lemon juice over the bananas.

~ Remove the pan with the rum from the heat, then set light to the rum with a match. Pour the flaming rum gently over the bananas and serve immediately.

Breads and Cakes

CORNMEAL DUMPLINGS ~ Trinidad

SWEET CORN BREAD ~ Dominican Republic

COCONUT BREAD ~ Barbados

BANANA BREAD ~ Jamaica

CASSAVA BISCUITS ~ Barbados

COCONUT SUGAR CAKES ~ Antigua

BAKES ~ Trinidad

GÂTEAU DE PATATE ~ Haiti

CORN PONE ~ Barbados

CARIBBEAN CHRISTMAS PUDDING ~ All the Islands

Trinidad

Cornmeal Dumplings

MAKES 12 DUMPLINGS

50 g/2 oz yellow cornmeal
50 g/2 oz plain flour
1 tsp baking powder
1½ tsp salt
40 g/1½ oz butter or margarine
3 tbsp cold water

~Sift the cornmeal, flour, baking powder and a quarter of the salt into a large mixing bowl. Mix well, then rub in the butter or margarine until the mixture looks like breadcrumbs. Add just enough of the water to make a dough.

~Divide the dough into 12 equal amounts and pat them into round dumplings.

~Bring 1.75 l/3 pt of water, to which 1 teaspoon of salt has been added, to the boil. Drop the dumplings into the water and stir once or twice to prevent them sticking to the bottom of the pan. Reduce the heat and simmer for 15 minutes or until the dumplings swell and rise to the surface.

~Remove them to a warmed serving dish.

~Serve at once with chicken stew.

***Above** Nutmegs drying.*

Dominican Republic

Sweet Corn Bread

MAKES 2 LOAVES

165 g/5½ oz butter or margarine
150 g/5 oz plain flour
375 g/13 oz yellow cornmeal
2 tsp baking powder
½ tsp ground cinnamon
½ tsp freshly ground nutmeg
½ tsp ground cloves
6 tbsp coconut milk (see page 15)
6 tbsp milk
50 g/2 oz sugar
4 eggs
200 g/7 oz fresh coconut meat, grated

~Preheat the oven to 200°C/400°F/Gas Mark 6.

~Use 15 g/½ oz of the butter or margarine to grease two 18 × 10 × 7.5-cm/7 × 4 × 3-in bread tins. Shake a little flour in each tin to coat.

~Sift the remaining flour, cornmeal, baking powder, cinnamon, nutmeg and cloves together. Gradually mix in the coconut milk and milk.

~Cream the remaining butter or margarine with the sugar until it is light and fluffy. Beat in the eggs, one at a time. Gradually incorporate the cornmeal mixture and coconut.

~Pour the batter into the prepared tins and bake in the centre of the preheated oven for 35 minutes or until golden brown.

~Leave to cool in the tins for 5 minutes, then turn the loaves out onto wire racks to cool completely.

***Right** Sweet Corn Bread.*

Barbados

Coconut Bread

MAKES 3 SMALL LOAVES

65 g/2½ oz butter or margarine
550 g/1¼ lb plain flour
400 g/14 oz caster sugar
2 tsp baking powder
½ tsp ground cinnamon
¼ tsp ground cloves
¾ tsp salt
1 large, fresh coconut, meat removed and finely grated
450 ml/15 fl oz milk

~Preheat the oven to 180°C/350°F/Gas Mark 4.

~Use 15 g/½ oz of the butter or margarine to grease three 9 × 18-cm/3½ × 7-in bread tins. Shake a little flour in each tin to coat.

~Sift the remaining flour, sugar, baking powder, cinnamon, cloves and salt into a deep mixing bowl. Add the grated coconut and mix everything together. Gradually incorporate the milk and remaining butter or margarine.

~Divide the batter between the prepared tins, filling each one not more than two-thirds full, then bake in the centre of the preheated oven for 1 hour or until the top is golden brown and crusty.

~Leave the loaves to cool in their tins for 5 minutes, then turn them out onto wire racks to cool completely.

114

Jamaica

Banana Bread

MAKES 1 LARGE LOAF

120 g/4½ oz butter or margarine
50 g/2 oz unsalted, shelled peanuts or blanched almonds
25 g/1 oz raisins
225 g/8 oz plain flour
2½ tsp baking powder
¼ tsp freshly ground nutmeg
½ tsp salt
2 large, ripe bananas
½ tsp vanilla essence
75 g/3 oz caster sugar
1 egg

~Preheat the oven to 180°C/350°F/Gas Mark 4.

~Use 15 g/½ oz of the butter or margarine to grease a 23 × 13 × 7.5-cm/9 × 5 × 3-in bread tin.

~Chop the nuts and mix them with the raisins.

~Sift the flour, baking powder, nutmeg and salt together.

~Peel the bananas and coarsely chop them, then mash to a purée with a fork. Add the vanilla essence.

~Cream the remaining butter or margarine with the sugar in a large mixing bowl. Blend in the egg. Beat the flour and banana mixtures in alternately. Beat well until the batter is smooth.

~Add the nut and raisin mixture.

~Pour the batter into the prepared tin. Bake in the preheated oven for 60 minutes.

~Leave the bread to cool in the tin for 5 minutes, then turn it out onto a wire rack to cool completely.

Right Banana Bread.

Barbados

Cassava Biscuits

MAKES 24

450g/1 lb cassava
100 g/4 oz butter or margarine
75 g/3 oz caster sugar
1 egg
150 g/5 oz fresh coconut meat, grated
225 g/8 oz plain flour
1 tsp baking powder

~Preheat the oven to 200°C/400°F/Gas Mark 6.

~Peel the cassava and grate the flesh. Squeeze off the juice (see page 15) and put the pulp to one side.

~Cream the butter or margarine and sugar together.

~Add the egg, grated cassava and coconut and mix together well.

~Mix the flour and baking powder together and sift them onto a sheet of greaseproof paper. Turn the creamed mixture out on to the paper and knead to incorporate the flour. When the dough is stiff, knead it for 2 or 3 more minutes, then roll it out to a thickness of about 2.5 cm/1 in. Using a floured 5-cm/ 2-in biscuit cutter, cut out the biscuits and place them on a baking tray about 2.5 cm/ 1 in apart. Bake in the preheated oven for 20 minutes or until the biscuits are golden brown.

Left Cassava Biscuits.

Antigua

Coconut Sugar Cakes

MAKES 15 CAKES

450 g/1 lb sugar
150 ml/5 fl oz water
drop of red, yellow or green food colouring (optional)
225 g/8 oz fresh coconut meat, grated
2 drops almond essence

~Boil the sugar in the water until the sugar has dissolved. Add the food colouring, coconut and almond essence, stirring all the time until the mixture becomes thick.

~Remove the pan from the heat and beat the mixture for a few minutes.

~Drop spoonfuls of the mixture onto a greased baking sheet. Leave to cool and harden.

117

Trinidad

Bakes

Fried Biscuits

MAKES 9 BISCUITS

225 g/8 oz plain flour
1½ tsp baking powder
1 tsp salt
25 g/1 oz butter, softened, or margarine
1½ tsp sugar dissolved in 3 tbsp cold water
vegetable oil for frying

~Sift the flour, baking powder and salt into a bowl. Add the butter or margarine and rub together until the mixture looks like breadcrumbs.

~Pour the sugar and water mixture into the bowl and mix to make a dough.

~Form the dough into small balls and flatten each into rounds about 7.5 cm/3 in in diameter.

~Heat a little oil in a large frying pan and fry the biscuits for about 3 minutes on each side. Transfer them to kitchen paper to drain.

118

Gateau de Patate

Sweet Potato Bread

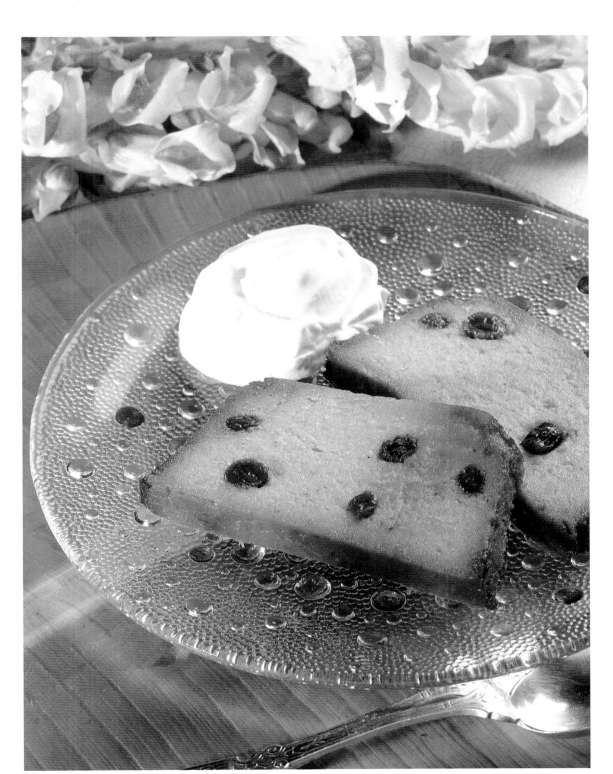

SERVES 6

65 g/2½ oz butter or margarine
850 g/2 lb sweet potatoes, peeled and quartered
1 large, ripe banana, peeled and chopped
3 eggs, lightly beaten
225 g/8 oz sugar
90 ml/3¼ fl oz milk
175 g/6 oz golden syrup
90 ml/3¼ fl oz evaporated milk
¼ tsp vanilla essence
¼ tsp freshly ground nutmeg
¼ tsp ground cinnamon
25 g/1 oz raisins

~ Preheat the oven to 180°C/350°F/Gas Mark 4.

~ Use 15 g/½ oz of the butter or margarine to grease a 23 × 13 × 7.5-cm/9 × 5 × 3-in bread tin.

~ Boil the sweet potatoes in salted water until soft, then drain and mash them with a fork.

~ Mash the banana pieces and mix with the sweet potato in a deep bowl.

~ Add the remaining butter, eggs, sugar, milk, golden syrup, evaporated milk, vanilla, nutmeg, cinnamon and raisins to the bowl and beat well.

~ Pour the batter into the prepared tin and bake in the preheated oven for 1½ hours.

~ Leave to cool for 5 minutes in the tin and then turn it on to a wire rack to cool completely.

~ Serve with fresh cream.

119

Corn Pone

Cornmeal Cake with Raisins and Cherries

SERVES 8

225 g/8 oz butter or margarine
250 g/9 oz yellow cornmeal
225 g/8 oz plain flour
225 g/8 oz sugar
¼ tsp vanilla essence
¼ tsp freshly ground nutmeg
pinch of salt
6 eggs, lightly beaten
300 ml/10 fl oz milk
1 tbsp light rum
150 g/5 oz raisins

~ Preheat the oven to 180°C/350°F/Gas Mark 4.

~ Use 15 g/½ oz of the butter or margarine to grease a 20-cm/8-in round cake tin.

~ Sift the cornmeal and flour together into a deep mixing bowl.

~ Cream the remaining butter or margarine and sugar together. Add this to the cornmeal mixture, together with the remaining ingredients, and mix well until the batter is smooth.

~ Pour the batter into the prepared tin and bake in the preheated oven for 1½ hours or until the cake is golden brown. Leave it to cool for 5 minutes before turning it out of the tin and serving.

120

Carribbean Christmas Pudding

MAKES 2 PUDDINGS

225 g/8 oz raisins
225 g/8 oz currants
225 g/8 oz prunes, chopped
100 g/4 oz mixed peel
175 g/6 oz glace cherries
1 tsp freshly grated nutmeg
1 tsp ground cinnamon
225 g/8 oz fresh, soft, white breadcrumbs
450 g/1 lb plain flour
1 tsp baking powder
225 g/8 oz sugar
225 g/8 oz butter or margarine
300 ml/10 fl oz brandy
2 tsp vanilla essence
1 tsp almond essence
50 ml/2 fl oz orange juice
150 ml/5 fl oz milk
175 g/6 oz ground almonds
50 g/2 oz ground cashew nuts
6 eggs, beaten

~ In a large mixing bowl combine the raisins, currants, prunes, mixed peel, glacé cherries, nutmeg, cinnamon and breadcrumbs.

~ Add the flour, baking powder, sugar and butter or margarine and mix them together well.

~ Add the brandy, essences and orange juice. Mix again and leave to stand overnight.

~ Next day, add the milk, nuts and eggs.

~ Pour the mixture into two 22 × 13 × 8 cm/ 9 × 5 × 3 in pudding bowls that have been well greased and lined with greaseproof paper. Seal the bowls tightly with a tea towel tied round them to prevent water getting in. Place each pudding in a saucepan of boiling water, cover and steam for 3 hours.

~ When done, remove the bowls from the saucepans and leave to cool.

~ Remove the puddings from the bowls and wrap in greaseproof paper, then in foil. Before serving, reheat conventionally or in a microwave and serve with whipped cream or brandy butter.

Right *Caribbean Christmas Pudding.*

Indo-Caribbean Dishes

ROTI ~ Trinidad

GOAT CURRY ~ Jamaica

CHOKA ~ Guyana

SAHINA ~ Trinidad

POLOURI ~ Trinidad

CHICKEN PELAU ~ Trinidad

CRAB PELAU ~ Tobago

KACHOURI ~ Trinidad

BAIGANI ~ Trinidad

CURRIED LAMB WITH LENTILS ~ Surinam and Trinidad

Dhalpouri or Roti

Indian Bread Stuffed with Split Pea Purée

The Indian influence shows itself more in the cuisine of Jamaica, Trinidad, Guyana and Surinam than it does in the cuisines of the other islands. Curry has become an integral part of Caribbean cooking and, indeed, the national party dish of Jamaica is curried goat and rice. Rice and chicken curry or goat curry must be on the menu at every party! In Trinidad, pelau is the national dish. It is a beautiful saffron-coloured rice dish with meat or seafood and is garnished with raisins and tomatoes.

SERVES 10

450 g/1 lb split peas
1 tbsp salt
½ tsp ground turmeric
1 tbsp cumin seeds
¼ tsp chilli powder (optional)
750 g/1½ lb plain flour
6 tsp baking powder
50 g/2 oz ghee (clarified butter) or margarine
vegetable oil for frying

~Wash the split peas and put them in a saucepan full of water to which half of the salt and the turmeric have been added. Bring to the boil and cook for 10 minutes or until the split peas are half-cooked.

~Drain off the water and process the split peas in a blender or food processor to form a powder, not a paste.

~Add the cumin and chilli then set the mixture on one side.

~Sift the flour, the remaining salt and the baking powder into a large mixing bowl.

~Mix in the ghee or margarine, working it in until it is well blended.

~Add just enough warm water, little by little, until you have a soft dough. Knead the dough for 5 minutes.

~Form the dough into small balls and set aside on a floured board. Flour your hands well and flatten the balls into thick rounds. Put 1 or 2 tablespoons of the split pea mixture into the centre of each round and close the dough over it, making sure the split pea mixture is sealed inside the dough. Then, roll each with a floured rolling pin on a floured board to make a circle about 12 cm/4¾ in in diameter and 2 cm thick.

~Brush the tops with oil and place them, oiled side down, on a hot griddle. Cook them for 3 minutes, brush their tops with oil and turn over. Cook both sides until they are lightly browned. Remove them to a clean tea towel and wrap to keep them warm.

~Serve with fish, meat, chicken or vegetable curry.

124

Jamaica

Goat Curry

SERVES 6

1.5 kg/3 lb goat meat, chopped
1 tbsp salt
3 garlic cloves, crushed
1 tbsp vinegar or 2 tbsp lime or lemon juice
50 ml/2 fl oz vegetable oil
1 onion, sliced
1/2 tsp ground cumin
50 g/2 oz curry powder
1 large, fresh tomato, chopped
1 fresh hot pepper, sliced (see page 16)
pinch methi leaves, chopped, to garnish (optional)

~Put the goat meat into a glass bowl together with the salt, half the garlic, the vinegar or lime or lemon juice and 2 tablespoons of cold water. Mix them together well and leave to marinate for 3 hours.

~Heat the oil in a large saucepan over a medium heat. Add the onion and remaining garlic and fry for 2 minutes until golden brown.

~Add the cumin and curry powder, mixed in a little water, and cook for 2 more minutes.

~Add the meat and sauté for 5 minutes.

~Add the tomato and hot pepper and bring to the boil. Lower the heat and simmer until the meat is tender.

~Garnish with chopped methi leaves.

~Serve with steamed rice.

Guyana

Choka

Aubergine Chutney

SERVES 6

2 medium aubergines
2 garlic cloves
2 tbsp olive oil
1 onion, finely chopped
juice of 1/2 lemon or lime
1 fresh hot pepper, finely chopped
2 spring onions, chopped
salt and freshly ground black pepper

~Wash the aubergines and cut a 2.5 cm/1 in slit in each one. Slot a clove of garlic into each hole. Rub the aubergines with some olive oil and place them under a hot grill, cooking them until the skin is black and the flesh soft and mushy. Discard the garlic cloves. Remove the aubergines to a plate and leave to cool.

~Peel off the skins and mash the flesh with a fork.

~Add the remaining olive oil, onion, lemon or lime juice, hot pepper, spring onions and salt and freshly ground black pepper to taste. Mix thoroughly.

~Serve with rice and chicken or fish curry.

127

Left Goat Curry.

Sahina

Dasheen Leaf Fritters

MAKES 12

6 dasheen leaves or spinach leaves, washed
225 g/¹/₂ lb split pea meal
125 g/4 oz plain flour
1 tsp baking powder
1 tsp ground turmeric
pinch of salt
250 ml/8 fl oz cold water
vegetable oil for frying

~Leave the leaves to dry for a few days until they have turned slightly brown.

~In a bowl, mix the split pea meal, flour, baking powder, turmeric and salt. Mix well, then add the water gradually to form a smooth batter.

~Spread some batter over each leaf and stack them on top of each other. When the stack is 8–10 cm/3–4 in thick (about 6 leaves), roll the leaves up along the longest edge like a Swiss roll and slice the roll across.

~Heat a little oil in a large frying pan and fry the slices until they are crisp. Remove them to some kitchen paper to drain.

~Serve with hot pepper sauce.

128

Above *Cattle and egrets, Trinidad.*

Polouri

Split Pea Fritters

MAKES 50

450 g/1 lb split pea meal
225 g/¹/₂ lb plain flour
1 tsp baking powder
¹/₂ tsp ground turmeric
¹/₂ tsp salt
120 ml/4 fl oz cold water
vegetable oil for frying

~In a bowl mix the split pea meal, flour, baking powder, turmeric and salt.

~Add the water gradually, mixing well, to form a smooth batter.

~Heat enough oil in a large frying pan to deep-fry the fritters.

~Drop spoonfuls of the batter into the oil and fry for 5 minutes until they are golden brown. Remove the polouris and allow to drain on kitchen paper. Serve either hot or cold.

Right *Polouri.*

Trinidad

Chicken Pelau

Chicken with Rice and Pigeon Peas

SERVES 6

1 onion, chopped
2 garlic cloves
1 tbsp chopped fresh chives
1 tbsp chopped fresh thyme
2 celery sticks with leaves, chopped
4 tbsp water
fresh coconut meat from ¹/₂ coconut (see page 15), chopped
liquid from fresh coconut (see page 15)
450 g/1 lb tin pigeon peas, drained
1 fresh hot pepper
1 tsp salt
freshly ground black pepper
2 tbsp vegetable oil
2 tbsp sugar
1.5 kg/3¹/₂ lb chicken, chopped
225 g/8 oz uncooked rice, washed and drained
300 ml/¹/₂ pt water

~Grind the onion, garlic, chives, thyme and celery with 4 tablespoons water in a blender or food processor. Empty the mixture into a large saucepan.

~Make coconut milk using the coconut meat and liquid.

~Add the coconut milk to the pan, together with the pigeon peas and hot pepper. Cook over a low heat for 15 minutes, then season with the salt and freshly ground black pepper to taste.

~Heat the oil in a flameproof casserole. Add the sugar and heat until it begins to caramelize.

~Add the raw chicken to the casserole and cook for 15 minutes until it has browned. Stir in the pigeon pea mixture, rice and 300 ml/¹/₂ pt of water. Bring to the boil, reduce the heat, cover and simmer for 20 minutes or until the rice and chicken are cooked. Discard the hot pepper before serving.

Tobago

Crab Pelau

Rice with Crab and Coconut Milk

SERVES 6

25 g/1 oz butter or margarine
2 tbsp vegetable oil
1 medium onion, chopped
1 garlic clove, chopped
¹/₂ tsp hot pepper, chopped (see page 16)
5 tsp curry powder
375 g/13 oz uncooked long-grain white rice, washed
900 ml/1¹/₂ pt coconut milk (see page 15)
1 tsp salt
freshly ground black pepper
450 g/1 lb fresh, tinned or frozen crabmeat
1 tbsp fresh lime
2 tbsp raisins

~Melt the butter or margarine in a large saucepan over a medium heat. Add the oil, onion, garlic and hot pepper and cook for 5 more minutes.

~Add the curry powder and stir in, then add the rice and cook for 3 minutes.

~Add the coconut milk, salt and freshly ground black pepper to taste and bring to the boil over a high heat, then reduce the heat, cover and simmer for 15 minutes.

~Add the crabmeat and lime or lemon juice and simmer for 5 more minutes or until the liquid has been absorbed. Decorate with the raisins and serve hot.

~Serve with a cucumber salad.

131

Left *Chicken Pelau.*

Kachouri

Chickpea Fritters

MAKES 20

450 g/1 lb gram or chickpea dhal
4 spring onions, chopped
1/2 hot pepper, chopped
1 tsp baking powder
pinch of salt
vegetable oil for frying

~Soak the dhal in water overnight.

~Next day, drain off the water and grind the dhal to a paste in a blender or food processor. Transfer the paste to a mixing bowl.

~Add the spring onions, hot pepper, baking powder and salt and mix them well.

~Shape the mixture into small balls. Heat enough oil in a large frying pan to deep-fry the fritters until they are golden brown. Remove them to kitchen paper to drain.

132

Baigani

Aubergine Fritters

SERVES 6

850 g/2 lb aubergines or potatoes
1 tbsp salt
85 g/3 1/4 oz plain flour
freshly ground black pepper
4 spring onions, chopped
1/2 hot pepper, chopped
120 ml/4 fl oz cold water
vegetable oil for frying

~Cut the aubergines into 1 cm/1/2 in thick slices and layer in a colander, sprinkling a little of the salt over each layer, then leave, weighted down with a plate, for 20 minutes. Rinse off the bitter juices and pat dry with kitchen paper.

~If using potatoes instead, simply slice thinly .

~In a large mixing bowl, put the flour, black pepper, spring onions, hot pepper and a pinch of salt and mix well.

~Gradually add the water to the bowl to make a smooth batter.

~Heat enough oil in a large frying pan to deep-fry the aubergine or potato slices.

~Dip the aubergine or potato slices in the batter and deep-fry until they are golden brown. Remove to kitchen paper to drain, then serve hot.

~Serve with tomato or coconut chutney.

Curried Lamb with Lentils

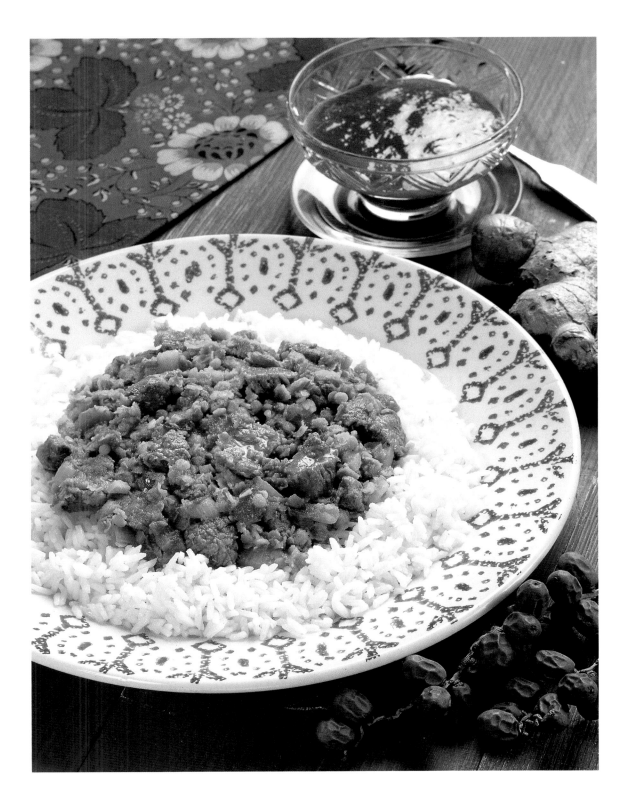

SERVES 6

2 tbsp oil
1 tbsp cumin seeds
1 tsp ground turmeric
1 large onion, chopped
2 garlic cloves, crushed
5 cm/2 in length of root ginger, peeled and finely chopped
850 g/2 lb boned lamb or goat meat, cubed
1 hot pepper, chopped
225 g/8 oz lentils, washed and drained
400 g/14 oz tin tomatoes, drained and chopped
1 tsp salt
freshly ground black pepper
600 ml/1 pt cold water

133

~ Heat the oil in a flameproof casserole, then add the cumin, turmeric, onion, garlic and ginger. Fry them for 5 minutes over a medium heat.

~ Add the lamb or goat meat and cook for 5 more minutes.

~ Stir in the hot pepper, lentils, tomatoes, salt and freshly ground black pepper to taste. Add the cold water, bring to the boil, then lower the heat, cover and simmer for 1 hour until the lamb or goat is tender and the sauce has become thick.

~ Serve with Roti (see page 124) or steamed rice and mango chutney.

Drinks

Peanut Punch

Pina Colada

Banana Daiquiri

Mawby

Rum Daisy

Passion Fruit Cocktail

Sorrel

Bossa Nova

Soursop Nectar

Ginger Beer

Peanut Punch

SERVES 4

75 g/3 oz smooth peanut butter or 225 g/8 oz roasted
peanuts, finely ground
400 g/14 oz tin evaporated milk
400 g/14 oz tin condensed milk
250 ml/8 fl oz water
1 tbsp sugar (optional)
1 egg
rind of 1 lime or lemon
1 tsp vanilla essence
475 ml/16 fl oz white rum or 250 ml/8 fl oz milk
(optional)

~ Mix the peanut butter or ground peanuts with the evaporated milk.

~ Add the condensed milk and water and mix together well. Taste and, if it is not sweet enough, add the sugar.

~ Beat the egg with the lime or lemon rind, then discard the rind.

~ Add the egg mixture, vanilla and rum or milk to the peanut and milk mixture.

~ Bottle and chill.

~ Serve with ice cubes.

Pina Colada

SERVES 2

25 g/1 oz coconut cream
40 ml/1½ fl oz rum
85 ml/3 fl oz unsweetened pineapple juice
150 ml/5 fl oz crushed ice
2 slices pineapple to decorate
2 cherries to decorate

~ Blend all the ingredients, except the pineapple and cherries, together in a blender for 10 seconds.

~ Serve in tall glasses with a straw, decorated with pineapple slices and cherries.

Banana Daiquiri

SERVES 4

juice of ½ lime or lemon
1 tsp sugar
75 g/3 oz banana, tinned mango or pineapple, chopped
50 ml/2 fl oz white rum
12 ice cubes, crushed
4 cherries to decorate

~ Blend all the ingredients, except the cherries, together with the ice.

~ Serve in cocktail glasses decorated with cherries on cocktail sticks.

Left *Peanut Punch.*
Right *Pina Colada.*

136

Mawby

SERVES 10

100 g/4 oz mawby bark
3 bay leaves
1.8 l/3¼ pt cold water
white sugar to sweeten

~Put the mawby bark, bay leaves and cold water into a large saucepan. Bring to the boil, then lower the heat and simmer for 10 minutes.

~Leave to stand until it has cooled completely.

~Strain out the bark and bay leaves and refrigerate the liquid in bottles for use as required.

~To prepare the drink, make a syrup by combining sugar and cold water, heat until the sugar dissolves and cool again. Add some of the refrigerated soursop mixture and serve with ice cubes. If you want the drink less bitter, just add less of the mawby mixture to the syrup.

Rum Daisy

SERVES 2

30 ml/1 fl oz white rum
juice of ½ lemon
1 tbsp grenadine syrup
2 cherries to decorate
2 slices banana to decorate

~Mix the liquid ingredients together and decorate the glasses with cherries and banana slices.

Passion Fruit Cocktail

SERVES 6

50 ml/2 fl oz sherry
1.2 l/2 pt passion fruit juice
2 tsp Angostura Bitters
250 ml/8 fl oz grapefruit juice
250 ml/8 fl oz guava juice
250 ml/8 fl oz lemon juice
250 ml/8 fl oz rum
900 g/3½ oz brown sugar

1 nutmeg, freshly grated
1 orange, thinly sliced
6 cherries to decorate

~Blend all the ingredients, except for the nutmeg, orange slices and cherries, together. Serve in tall glasses decorated with a slice of orange, a cherry and a sprinkling of grated nutmeg.

Sorrel

SERVES 10

450 g/1 lb fresh sorrel leaves or 100 g/4 oz dry
sorrel leaves
2 bay leaves
3 whole cloves
1 small cinnamon stick
850 g/2 lb white sugar

~Put the sorrel and bay leaves, cloves,
cinnamon and sugar into a large saucepan.
Pour hot water over to cover the leaves and
boil for 1 minute only.

~Remove the pan from the heat and leave to
cool. Leave to stand overnight.

~Next day, sieve out the leaves and spices and
sweeten to taste, if necessary. Bottle and put
1 whole clove in each bottle. Cap the bottles
and leave to stand for 4 days. Chill and serve
with ice cubes.

Opposite *Passion Fruit Cocktail.*
Left *Sorrel.*

Bossa Nova

SERVES 2

30 ml/1 fl oz dark rum
8 ml/¼ fl oz lime juice
8 ml/¼ fl oz lemon juice
15 ml/½ fl oz passion fruit juice
2 slices orange to decorate
2 slices lime to decorate

~Shake all the ingredients, except the orange and lime slices, together well and serve in tumblers with crushed ice, decorated with slices of orange and lime.

Soursop Nectar

SERVES 4

1 large soursop
250 ml/8 fl oz cold water
250 ml/8 fl oz milk or single cream
200 g/7 oz sugar

~Peel the soursop and put the pulp, together with the seeds, into a big sieve over a bowl. Press it with a spoon until all the liquid has been pressed out of the pulp and into the bowl.

~Pour the water, milk or cream, sugar and soursop liquid into a blender and blend for 10 seconds.

~If the nectar is too sweet, add some more milk or cream and a drop of lime or lemon juice.

~Serve chilled.

Ginger Beer

SERVES 6

100 g/4 oz piece fresh root ginger
juice of 1 lime or lemon
3 whole cloves
850 g/2 lb sugar
1.75 l/4 pt water

~ Peel the root ginger and slice it thinly.

~ Put the ginger slices, together with the lime or lemon juice, cloves and sugar in the cold water in a saucepan, bring to the boil and boil for 5 minutes.

~ Remove the pan from the heat and leave to stand overnight.

~ The next day, sieve and taste it. If it is not sweet enough, add more sugar; if it is too sweet, add more water. Bottle the ginger beer, adding a whole clove to each bottle. Cap the bottles and leave them to stand for 5 days. Chill and serve with ice cubes.

Left *Bossa Nova.*

Index

143

Picture Credits

Quarto would like to thank the following for providing photographs and for permission to reproduce copyright material. While every effort has been made to acknowledge all copyright holders, we would like to apologize should any omissions have been made.

p4: John Dakers/Life File; *p9:* Grenada Board of Tourism; *p11:* Juliet Highet/Life File; *p12:* Allan Gordon/Life File; *p13:* Jeremy Hoare/Life File; *p14:* Andy Kidd/Life File; *p18:* Paul Richards/Life File; *p30:* Juliet Highet/Life File; *p34:* Andy Teare/Life File; *p38:* Peter Phipp/ Travel Pictures; *p42:* Juliet Highet/Life File; *p54:* Paul Richards/Life File; *p64:* George Leaney/Life File; *p66:* Grahame A Singleton/Life File; *p72:* Lionel Moss/Life File; *p80:* Grenada Board of Tourism; *p86:* Jeremy Hoare/Life File; *p92:* Peter Phipp/Travel Pictures; *p94:* Jeremy Hoare/Life File; *p103:* Paul Richards/Life File; *p104:* Peter Phipp/ Travel Pictures; *p110:* Peter Phipp/Travel Pictures; *p112:* Grenada Board of Tourism; *p122:* Peter Phipp/Travel Pictures; *p128:* George Leaney/Life File; *p134:* Paul Richards/Life File.